My Dog Says
I'm a Great Cook!™

My Dog Says

I'm a Great Cook!™

By the Publishers, Readers, and Fans of

DogTipper.com

Visit us Online!
Visit www.DogTipper.com

ISBN: 978-0-9717620-1-5

Printed in the United States of America

Disclaimer

This book has been written to provide information to help you make treats for your dog for the purpose of saving money on your dog's care and living a better life with your dog. Every effort has been made to make this book as complete and accurate as possible. However, mistakes happen.

The purpose of this book is to educate and entertain. The authors and publisher do not warrant that the information contained in this guide is fully complete and shall not be responsible for any errors or omissions. The authors, contributors, and publisher shall have neither liability nor responsibility to any person or entity with respect to any loss or damage caused or alleged to be caused directly or indirectly by this report.

This book in no way replaces specific nutritional advice from your veterinarian. If you have any concerns at all about your dog's health, please make an appointment with your vet, and have him examined by a professional.

If you do not wish to be bound by the above, please return this book for a full refund.

Table of Contents

To the readers of DogTipper.com
who shared not only their dog treat recipes
but also the love that they have for their dogs!

Introduction

Preparing food for those we love is one of the most basic ways to show how much we care. The act of cooking for our families—including our four-legged family members—shares our love and nurtures those we hold dear.

And, we have to admit, cooking for dogs is good for our egos as chefs! If those bone-shaped cookies come out of the oven looking a little less than artistic, our dogs don't mind one bit. Canine cupcakes stuck to the pan? They taste just as good in pieces!

We love cooking for our dogs Tiki and Irie not only for the joy we get in watching them taste our homemade treats but also as a fun way to save money and control just what goes into our treats. Careful shopping lets us take advantage of sales and, at the same time, prepare treats that showcase seasonal fruits and vegetables. We know just what goes into the manufacture of our treats and exactly where the treats were made.

When we put out the call for recipes for this book, the reaction from our readers and fans was immediate. We received many recipes and photos and pared them down to those you see in this volume. We enjoyed reading about each and every dog lucky enough to live with a pet parent who delights in preparing homemade treats just for him or her.

Reading about the love these pet parents share with their dogs was, for us, the biggest treat of all.

> — Paris Permenter and John Bigley
> DogTipper.com

Foods Your Dog Should Never Eat

Although making your own dog treats can be a healthy and economical way to feed your dog, you must know which foods to never feed your dog. Among others, these are foods you must NOT feed your dog:

- ❖ Apricot pits
- ❖ Avocados
- ❖ Alcohol
- ❖ Apple seeds
- ❖ Cherry pits
- ❖ Chocolate
- ❖ Coffee (and other caffeinated drinks)
- ❖ Garlic: some people feed small amounts but only in moderation. Ask your vet for recommendations.
- ❖ Grapes and raisins: because they are condensed, raisins are more dangerous than grapes; avoid cereals and cookies with raisins.
- ❖ Macadamia nuts
- ❖ Onions
- ❖ Peach pits
- ❖ Persimmons: the seeds can cause problems
- ❖ Plum pits
- ❖ Potato peels: discard the peel and any green portions of the potato.
- ❖ Tea
- ❖ Yeast dough: uncooked dough is very dangerous to your dog.
- ❖ Xylitol: used in some diet foods and sugar-free gums, it is highly toxic to dogs.

Dehydrated Treats

Dehydrated Calf Liver
Contributed by S. Gilbert

1 pound calf liver

❖ Cut the calf liver in strips and place on the dehydrator tray. When placing on the tray, space the strips apart so they are not touching.

❖ Set dehydrator at 160 degrees F.

❖ Dehydrating time: 6-8 hours. (This will vary between dehydrators and depends on the number of dehydrating trays in use.)

❖ Cool and refrigerate.

I make enough to last a couple of weeks. You can break the strips into smaller pieces for training.

Oven directions: Place liver strips on a cookie sheet with parchment paper. Bake at 160 degrees F for 6-8 hours. Cool then refrigerate.

Contributor's Note: I love using my dehydrator. I decided to try calf liver in the dehydrator. Schooner and Skipper kept whining by the dehydrator...finally it was time to try the calf liver. It was a big hit. Schooner and Skipper are six months apart. Skipper is our rescue dog. They are the best of friends. They love playing, romping and swimming together. They sleep side by side.

Schooner and Skipper LOVE my cooking.

Dehydrated Chicken Gizzards & Hearts
Contributed by S. Gilbert

1 - 2 pounds chicken gizzards & hearts

❖ Place the gizzards and hearts on the dehydrator trays. Space them out so they are not touching.

❖ Check after 4-5 hours. Dehydrating time will vary depending on your dehydrator and the number of trays you are using.

❖ Remove from dehydrator trays and cool completely. Store in a container and refrigerate.

If you do not have a dehydrator, you can make this in the oven on a cookie sheet. Oven should be set at the lowest temperature.

Contributor's Note: Your dogs will enjoy this treat. Mine love the treats! After the scare with chicken jerky, I decided to start making my own treats for them. I love using my dehydrator for making dog treats. It is so easy. It was the best investment I made. Schooner and Skipper love it. They will sit and sniff at the counter to see what I am making. Schooner and Skipper are Vizslas. Skipper is our rescue dog. Skipper was rescued at 6 months old. They are the best of friends. Schooner is 2-½ years old and Skipper is 2 years old. Schooner and Skipper love it when I cook for them.

Sweet Potatoes & Bananas
Contributed by DogTipper.com

2 medium-sized sweet potatoes
4 ripe bananas

- ❖ Peel the sweet potatoes, being careful to remove any green "eyes" and parts you find. (The green parts of potatoes are toxic to dogs.)

- ❖ Slice the potatoes as thinly as you can; the easiest way is with a mandolin slicer.

- ❖ Peel and slice the bananas to about ¼-inch thick. If you'd rather the slices be chewy, just slice them a little thicker.

- ❖ Arrange the slices on the dehydrating trays. Place sweet potatoes and bananas on separate trays so you can rearrange the trays depending on their drying speed. Don't allow the slices to touch one another or the edges won't dry properly.

- ❖ Dry the potatoes and the bananas about 14 hours (although this will vary by dehydrator.)

- ❖ Cool and refrigerate.

I would rather see the portrait of a dog that I know, than all the allegorical paintings they can show me in the world. ~ Samuel Johnson

Turkey Meatballs
Contributed by S. Gilbert

1 pound ground turkey

- ❖ Roll the ground turkey into balls.

- ❖ Place on the dehydrator tray.

Cleaning dehydrator racks is easiest if you soak them overnight.

- ❖ Dehydrator should be set at 160 degrees F.

- ❖ Dehydrate for 8 - 10 hours depending on the size of the meatballs.

- ❖ If you make a lot of the turkey meatballs freeze half for another time. I keep the turkey meatballs in the refrigerator.

You can make the turkey meatballs in the oven. Place the meatballs on a jellyroll pan or cookie sheet with parchment paper and bake at 160 degrees. Time: 8-10 hours.

I did not add any ingredients to the ground turkey. You could add vegetables or cheese if you like.

Schooner and Skipper love turkey meatballs.

Contributor's Note: I love to cook for my dogs. Schooner and Skipper love ground turkey. I love using my dehydrator on the weekends to make them treats for the week. Schooner and Skipper are 6 months apart in age. Skipper is our rescue dog. They are the best of friends...best brothers.

Apple Chicken Bites
Contributed by S. Gilbert

*1 pound uncooked chicken, deboned
1-2 apples*

Dehydrator instructions:

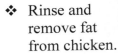

- ❖ Rinse and remove fat from chicken. Slice with the grain as thinly as possible, ⅛- to ¼-inch thick.
- ❖ Wash, core, and thinly slice apples.
- ❖ Take a slice of apple and chicken and wrap the chicken around the apple.
- ❖ You can wrap the chicken in the middle of the apple or just place a piece of chicken on top of the apple.
- ❖ Place on a dehydrator tray. I use a food dehydrator for making the Apple Chicken Bites; dehydrate about 8 - 10 hours. Check to make sure Bites are firm and dry.

Oven Instructions:

- ❖ Preheat oven to 200 degrees F. Lightly grease a baking sheet.
- ❖ Place the Apple Chicken Bites on the baking sheet.
- ❖ Bake for approximately 2 hours; jerky treats should be firm and dry, not at all soft or spongy. It is safer to go a little extra dry and firm than for the meat to be underdone.
- ❖ Remove from oven and cool on a wire rack until completely cool.

Contributor's Note: I started making the Apple Chicken Bites after finding out the brand I was buying for Schooner and Skipper was made in China. I now make my own for Schooner and Skipper. My Apple Chicken Bites do not have any preservatives added. I make just enough for a week at a time.

Schooner needed a brother so we rescued Skipper at 6 months old. Skipper will be two years old and Schooner is 2 ½ years old. They romp, play, sleep side by side, and love to snuggle.

I have found that when you are deeply troubled there are things you get from the silent devoted companionship of a dog that you can get from no other source. ~ Doris Day

Dehydrated Beef Heart Treats
Contributed by S. Gilbert

1 beef heart

❖ Cut in strips about ½-inch thick.

❖ Place strips on your dehydrator trays. Make sure the strips are not touching.

Regardless of the food you're dehydrating, don't crowd the dehydrator trays. Leave plenty of room for airflow for best results.

❖ Set dehydrator to 160 degrees. Dehydrate for 14-16 hours. (Contributor's note: I had mine on for 16 hours. You may choose to put your dehydrator in your garage or outside. I put my dehydrator outside. I was not sure I wanted the smell in the house.)

❖ I broke the long strips into much smaller pieces.

❖ Cool and put in a container and refrigerate.

Schooner and Skipper loved the Beef Heart. Great for training.

Note: You can make this recipe in the oven at 160 degrees. Place the strip on a cookie sheet with parchment paper.

Contributor's Note: I love using my dehydrator. I make treats every weekend for the week. It is so easy because I put chicken on one tray and chicken gizzards on another tray. I love trying all kind of recipes for my dogs. Schooner and Skipper love the jerky. I know what I am making is all natural and does not have all the preservatives added.

Jerky Treats

Tail-Waggin' Turkey Jerky
Contributed by Deanna Ray,
www.loveofmydogs.com

½ pound lean ground turkey
1 egg
½ cup oats
½ cup carrots, shredded
½ cup fresh parsley, chopped or 1 tablespoon dry parsley

❖ Preheat oven to 200 degrees F. Mix all ingredients together in large bowl. Add mixture to food processor and blend thoroughly. Spread mixture using a spatula about ¼-inch thick onto foil-lined cookie sheet. Bake for 1 hour.

❖ Remove from oven and cut jerky into strips 1-inch wide by 3 to 5 inches long (the length depends on your dog's size and will slightly alter the cooking time).

❖ Place strips onto larger foil-lined cookie sheet, spaced ½-inch apart, and return to oven for 1 hour. Remove from oven and use a spatula to loosen any jerky stuck to the foil. Return to oven for 1 hour or until hardened and very dry. Cool before serving. Store in refrigerator or airtight container.

Contributor's Note: Deanna is the creator of For the Love of My Dogs website (www.loveofmydogs.com) and blog featuring tips, stories and advice on all things dog. Included are informative resources on animal rescue and adoption, homemade dog-tested recipes and wellness info, shopping suggestions, training tips and more! Deanna's passions include rescuing animals, encouraging pet adoption and raising awareness to stop and prevent animal cruelty. Deanna volunteers at Miami-Dade Animal Services, fosters shelter pets and has three rescue dogs and a cat at home.

Chicken Jerky Strips
Contributed by Kat

1 ½ pounds boneless, skinless chicken breast tenders, sliced into strips
½ cup vegetable oil
1 tablespoon salt
Optional: seasonings such as parsley, rosemary, and sage*

❖ Slice tenders into strips about ¼- to ⅛-inch thick.

❖ Place the chicken breast strips in an even layer across the entire the tray, leaving an equal amount of space between pieces and making sure that they do not touch each other. This is so air can flow between them while they are drying out, which helps dehydrate them.

❖ Once the strips are all set out, place the trays in the food dehydrator, turn it on, and set the temperature for 140 degrees. It will probably take between 3 and 12 hours for the chicken to fully dry. (In an oven, bake the chicken strips at 200 degrees for approximately 2 hours.)

Contributor's Note: I have made these strips many times for my dog, Gwen. She adores them and they are healthy for her, too.

*Editors' note: Some practitioners warn that rosemary, sage, and other herbs may be detrimental to some dogs so adjust usage depending on your dog.

Chicken Jerky
Contributed by DogTipper.com

1 pound chicken breasts, deboned

- ❖ Preheat oven to 170-180 degrees F (depending on how low your oven will go).

- ❖ Slice chicken breasts in strips no more than ¼-inch thick. Slice with the grain of the chicken, rather than against it to make treats a little chewier.

- ❖ Place slices on a greased cookie sheet; be sure to use one with a slight edge because there will be water and juices from the chicken during the first hour of cooking. Leave about a ½-inch between slices.

- ❖ Bake for two hours. After two hours, check the slices and see if they're dry. (They should look like a very well-done French fry.)

- ❖ When they're done, remove the treats from the oven and cool on a drying rack. When the treats are completely cool, bag in zippered bags or pop them in an airtight container and refrigerate.

Dogs are our link to paradise. They don't know evil or jealousy or discontent. To sit with a dog on a hillside on a glorious afternoon is to be back in Eden, where doing nothing was not boring—it was peace.
~ Milan Kundera

Turkey Jerky Treats
Contributed by DogTipper.com

2 pounds lean ground turkey

- ❖ Preheat oven to 170 degrees F.

- ❖ Fill jerky gun with ground turkey and slowly squeeze out jerky onto baking screens with a drip tray below.

Jerky guns are sold with various attachments to create flat and tubular jerky. Along with baking the jerky, you can also cook in a dehydrator.

- ❖ Bake for 2 ½ hours. About half an hour before they're done, turn each of the pieces. Cool completely before refrigerating. These can be cut into training treat-size portions as well!

Fetching Savings on Meat Purchases

Meat prices are on the rise but with some careful savings you can economize to prepare high-quality dog treats on a budget. Savings tips include:

- ❖ Talk with wild game processors. During hunting season, wild game processors sometimes sell a mix for dogs; you can also obtain low-cost antlers and bones.

- ❖ Locate your local meat processing plants. Often you can save money by buying directly from meat processing plants in your area.

- ❖ Visit your local butcher. Make a stop by your local butcher (not the butcher in your supermarket who may receive meat pre-processed). Ask if he sells low-cost cuts, ones that aren't as attractive to customers but are protein-packed and economical options for dog treats.

- ❖ Buy an electric food grinder. Grinding meat is much less expensive than buying ground meat for treats; you can also cut away the fat to prepare a healthier treat.

- ❖ Band with raw feeders. Join up with raw feeders in your area to purchase large quantities of meat at a better price.

Biscuit Treats

Brody's Favorite Biscuits
Contributed by Tam Jam

2 cups Bisquick
Baking Mix
⅔ cup milk
¾ cup shredded
cheddar cheese
1 stick butter, melted
2 chicken breasts,
boiled and chopped

Did You Know?

Bisquick contains flour, shortening, salt, and baking powder. It was invented by a railway chef who needed a premix he could prepare in the train's small kitchen.

❖ Preheat oven to 450 degrees F.

❖ Combine all ingredients and then with a large spoon place onto greased cookie tray about 2 to 3 inches apart.

❖ Bake for 10 minutes. You will know they are done when they are golden brown.

Contributor's Note: Keep in mind these are human grade. You and I can eat them. We have a Wolf hybrid dog that is used to eating dinner remains. And he hardly ever eats dog food. Well recently I started cooking for him. Here is one of those things. Enjoy! I am a Ragdoll cat breeder. And have for the past year been studying cat diets and the best foods to feed them. I see now that it's best to just cook for pets. But most of us won't or don't or whatever. I like to cook for them now and then. I know at Thanksgiving the cats like the turkey more than we do! And so I share my food with them sometimes.

Rowdy's Homemade Biscuits
Contributed by Sasha's Mom

2 ⅓ cups whole wheat flour
½ cup non-fat dry milk
1 teaspoon sugar
1 teaspoon salt
6 tablespoons melted butter
1 egg
½ cup beef bouillon

❖ Preheat oven to 325 degrees F.

❖ Mix dry ingredients. Add melted butter, eggs, and liquid. Mix, then knead for 3 minutes.

❖ Roll the dough, ¼ to ½-inch thick.

❖ Cut out fun shapes with cookie cutters or simply roll the dough into rectangles and use a pizza cutter to make 1- to 1½-inch squares.

❖ Bake for 40-50 minutes, until fairly hard. Cool before storing or serving.

Contributor's Note: Sasha is very picky but enjoyed this recipe which was passed to me by a friend.

Histories are more full of examples of the fidelity of dogs than of friends. ~ Alexander Pope

Pumpkin PB Wafers
contributed by PetsWeekly,
www.petsweekly.com

15-ounce can pureed pure pumpkin (not filling)
¾ cup uncooked cream of wheat*
½ cup dry powdered milk
¼ cup creamy peanut butter

* If wheat sensitive, substitute rice cereal.

Did You Know?

Pumpkin is great for your dog's digestive system. It contains fiber for constipation and also will absorb excess water in the case of diarrhea.

❖ Preheat oven to 300 degrees F.

❖ Mix all ingredients together. Drop by the spoonful onto a lightly-greased cookie sheet

❖ Bake for 15-20 minutes.

Contributor's Note: PetsWeekly.com is written for the multi-pet household who treats their pets like family. We offer reliable product and service reviews on the newest pet products; as well as humorous stories, pet news, educational resources, animal facts, fun quotations, and helpful articles on behavioral and health concerns in pets of all species. Sit. Stay. And learn how to live amongst animals (without becoming one).

Peanut Butter Tasties
Contributed by Teddy's Momma

1 ½ cup whole wheat flour
1 cup quick oatmeal
1 cup creamy peanut butter
1 egg
1 tablespoon molasses
2 tablespoons olive oil
½ cup water
3 tablespoons Parmesan cheese (optional)

❖ Preheat oven to 350 degrees F.

❖ Mix all together, roll like cookie dough approximately ½-inch thick (using extra wheat flour to roll out). Cut into shapes with cookie cutters.

❖ Bake for 15 minutes, flip treats, bake additional 10-15 minutes.

❖ Cool treats completely. Keep in airtight container. (Can be refrigerated if kept longer than a week.)

Contributor's Note: My dog, Teddy, is a chow, and his skin reacts to treats and dog food that contains cornmeal, making him terribly itchy and uncomfortable. This recipe is one I have created for him. He loves them! And no reaction!

Bacon-Flavored Dog Biscuits
Contributed by MalibuGypsy

2 eggs
1 cup milk
½ cup water
1 teaspoon salt
10 tablespoons bacon fat, melted
5 cups whole wheat flour

❖ Preheat oven to 350 degrees F (175 degrees C).

❖ Lightly grease a cookie sheet. Beat eggs in a large bowl. Stir in milk, water, salt, and bacon fat until well blended. Gradually stir in flour to make a stiff dough. Pinch off pieces of the dough and roll into 2-inch balls. Place on prepared baking sheet.

❖ Bake in preheated oven for 35 to 40 minutes. Cool on racks.

❖ Store in a covered container in the refrigerator.

Contributor's Note: This recipe has been passed on by members of my dog-loving family! Our dogs love them!

Jiffy Mix Biscuits
Contributed by Rick

1 box muffin mix
1 egg
Olive oil

❖ Preheat oven to 400 degrees F or stated heat on mix package.

❖ Select your favorite Jiffy® Muffin Mix. Mine is Apple Cinnamon.

❖ Substitute all of the water or milk from muffin mix instruction with ¼ the amount of olive oil. If the recipe calls for 1 cup of milk, add ¼ cup of oil, but no milk.

❖ Add the egg. Mix, roll out flat, and cut with cookie cutters. Place in pan and bake for approximately 20 minutes. Keep an eye on them; you want them to be dried out and crispy, not burnt.

Contributor's Note: Crunchy bones are always the best, according to Tag! She always loved warm bones. So I would make them for her in small batches. In order to do that for her frequently, I used Jiffy® Mixes.

Heaven goes by favor. If it went by merit, you would stay out and your dog would go in. ~ Mark Twain

Good Dog, Bad Breath Muffins
Contributed by Melody McKinnon

Step 1: In one bowl blend:

> 4 cups rice flour or whole wheat flour (or a suitable wheat-free substitute)
> 1 tablespoon baking powder
> ½ teaspoon cinnamon (digestive aid)
> ¼ teaspoon ginger (soothes digestive system)
> 1 teaspoon powdered seaweed/algae (prebiotic and chlorophyll)
> ¼ teaspoon chlorella powder (chlorophyll)
> 1 teaspoon peppermint leaf powder or 3 drops peppermint essential oil (digestive aid & deodorizer)

Step 2: In a second bowl blend:

> 2 ½ cups water
> ½ teaspoon vanilla
> ¼ cup pure unsweetened applesauce (digestive aid)
> 1 cup plain, active yogurt (probiotics)
> 1 egg

Step 3: Blend the two bowls and then add:

> ¼ cup finely chopped or pureed fresh parsley (digestive aid & deodorizer)

Baking Instructions:

❖ Preheat oven: 350 degrees F.

❖ Pour into baking cups. Bake for about 45 minutes, then check every five minutes until a toothpick comes out clean.

❖ Reduce cooking time for mini baking cups.

Contributor's Note: Melody McKinnon writes for AllNaturalPetCare.com and other websites and publications. She has also developed Bottom Bites, an all-natural line of fish food. Melody holds 52 certifications revolving around nutrition, biochemistry, general sciences, business, marketing, design, and writing. She asks that you please support animal shelters and consider pet adoption.

Anybody who doesn't know what soap tastes like never washed a dog. ~ Franklin P. Jones

PB Bacon Dog Biscuits
Contributed by Malia R.,
www.BaylieDog.com

3 cups whole-wheat flour
2 eggs
1 cup peanut butter
⅓ cup low-fat milk
3 teaspoons bacon grease
2 slices bacon, cooked

- ❖ Preheat oven to 375 degrees F.

- ❖ In a bowl, combine flour and eggs. In another bowl, mix peanut butter, bacon grease, bacon (crumbled) and milk. Add wet mixture to dry, and mix well.

- ❖ Turn out dough on a lightly floured surface and knead. Roll out to ¼-inch thickness and cut out shapes.

- ❖ Place on a greased baking sheet and bake 20 minutes or until lightly brown. Cool on a rack and store in an airtight container in refrigerator.

Makes about 20-30 dog biscuits.

Contributor's Note: Baylie Dog gives this recipe a "thumbs up"… if she had thumbs. Visit www.BaylieDog.com

Dogs love company. They place it first in their short list of needs. ~ J.R. Ackerly

Mint Bones

Contributed by Misty

1 tablespoon olive oil
1 cup water
2 ½ cups flour
½ cup oatmeal
2 tablespoon fresh mint (or 2 teaspoons dried mint)
⅓ cup chopped parsley

- ❖ Preheat oven to 350 degrees F.

- ❖ Mix oil and water, slowly add flour and other ingredients. Roll dough out on a flat surface.

- ❖ Cut with bone-shaped cookie cutters or in small rectangles.

- ❖ Bake for 35 minutes. These treats freeze well, but last for about a month unfrozen.

Contributor's Note: Benefits of mint and parsley: The parsley and mint help refresh your pet's breath. Mint can be soothing to the stomach and nervous system and help alleviate nausea. Parsley is soothing and can help relieve arthritic pain.

No one appreciates the very special genius of your conversation as the dog does. ~ Christopher Morley

Maggie's Harvest Munchies
Contributed by Marsha Pay

½ cup oatmeal or barley flakes
2 cups rye or whole wheat flour
6 tablespoons oil
⅔ cup water
2 cloves minced garlic
½ cup roasted, unsalted sunflower seeds (coarsely chopped if you like)

❖ Preheat oven to 350 degrees F.

❖ Mix all ingredients using an electric mixer or food processor. Add a little water if dough seems dry. Roll dough out to about ¼ -inch thickness and cut into shapes. You can also roll into small balls and press flat with a fork.

❖ Bake for 35-40 minutes. Biscuits will harden more if you leave them overnight in the oven after you turn it off. Store at room temperature in a covered container.

Contributor's Note: Maggie taught me how to train dogs! She was my patient, loving pal who was happy to spend hours with me as I learned better methods for teaching beginner dogs new things. Maggie's gone now, but I continue to teach beginner classes at our local humane society, and at our local obedience club. Maggie, along with all her canine siblings through the years, made sure that all of our homemade treats were "Lab-tested"!

Apples and Oats
Contributed by Misty

2 large apples
½ cup honey
1 cup water
1 teaspoon cinnamon
2 cups oatmeal
3 cups all-purpose flour

- ❖ Preheat oven to 350 degrees F.

- ❖ Wash, core, and finely chop the apples. In a large bowl, mix the apples, honey, water, cinnamon, and oatmeal. Gradually add flour until dough is stiff.

- ❖ Either pitch off small amounts or use a small melon baller to make treat-sized balls of dough. Place on cookie sheet and flatten them out.

- ❖ Bake for 30 minutes. Remove tray and flip treats. Lower oven temperature to 325 degrees and bake another 30 minutes. This should give you evenly browned treats. Cool and store.

Contributor's Note: Crunchy apple treats! What could be better?

Oatmeal Yummies
Contributed by LJ Martin

1 ¼ cup flour
2 cups rice, cooked
½ cup quick oats
½ tablespoon brown gravy mix
¼ cup molasses
1 cup carrots, shredded
⅓ cup chopped spinach (fresh or frozen)
¼ cup applesauce
½ tablespoon vegetable oil

❖ Preheat oven to 350 degrees F.

❖ Mix dry and wet ingredients separately and slowly blend dry ingredients into the wet. Drop dough using a teaspoon onto greased cookie sheets.

❖ Bake until golden brown for 15- 20 minutes.

❖ Makes about 2 dozen cookies.

Contributor's Note: Loved by Duchess the cute Boston terrier.

To me, to live without dogs would mean accepting a form of blindness. ~ Thomas McGuane

Old-Fashioned Doggie Treats
Contributed by Paige Kelley

½ cup powdered milk
1 egg, well beaten
2 ½ cups flour
½ teaspoon garlic salt
1 ½ teaspoons brown sugar
½ cup water
6 tablespoons gravy
Baby food (your dog's favorite meat formula)

❖ Preheat oven to 350 degrees F.

❖ Mix all ingredients well. Roll out on a floured board to about ½-inch thick. Cut with floured cutters.

❖ Bake for 25-30 minutes. Cool. Cookies should be hard. Store in an airtight container.

Contributor's Note: This is the only recipe I've ever tried. All of my dogs love them!

My little dog—a heartbeat at my feet.
~ Edith Wharton

Basic Biscuits
Contributed by cstironkat

5 ½ cups whole wheat flour*
1 cup cornmeal
½ cup powdered milk
3 ½ cups beef, turkey or chicken broth**
2 tablespoons honey

* Or 3 cups unbleached flour and 2 ½ cups whole wheat flour
** If using canned broth, use low-sodium broth.

Did You Know?

Freeze extra broth in an ice tray. Broth cubes can be used as needed (or they make great dog treats!)

- ❖ Preheat oven to 350 degrees F.

- ❖ Mix all ingredients together and roll dough about ¼-inch thick. Cut into desired shapes.

- ❖ Bake for 15 minutes. Turn off oven and leave in oven overnight to harden.

Contributor's Note: These biscuits can be cut into holiday shapes for gift giving.

Happiness is a warm puppy.
~ Charles M. Schulz

Cheesy Biscuits
Contributed by Laura C

2 cups oat flour
½ cup olive oil
1 farm fresh egg
½ cup shredded cheese (your dog's favorite variety)
Water, to make the dough proper consistency

❖ Preheat oven to 350 degrees F.

❖ Mix the first three ingredients until smooth. Add cheese and water to make a cookie-like dough. Roll out on lightly floured surface.

❖ Cut biscuits into whatever shape you like. (I had dog bone-shaped cookie cutters.)

❖ Put onto greased cookie sheet and bake for ½ hour.

❖ Turn off the oven and leave biscuits in the oven until they cool down. This makes the biscuits crunchy. Enjoy!

Contributor's Note: Dogs are [generally] not allergic to oats. I found this out as my dog is allergic to both wheat and corn.

Veggie Bites
Contributed by cstironkat

1 egg, beaten
⅓ cup applesauce
1 cup cooked veggies (green beans, carrots, potatoes, sweet potatoes, or mixed veggies)
1 cup cooked brown rice
1 tablespoon brewers yeast
¾ cup cheddar cheese

- ❖ Preheat oven to 350 degrees F.

- ❖ Mix all ingredients. Drop teaspoons full on greased cookie sheet.

- ❖ Bake for 12 minutes for soft bites or turn off oven and leave the bites overnight or until oven cools for crunchy treats. Refrigerate.

Contributor's Note: I have made these for the birds without the cheese or yeast.

A dog has the soul of a philosopher. ~ Plato

Apple Cut-Outs
Contributed by cstironkat

2 cups whole wheat flour
½ cup rolled oats
1 apple, cored and grated
1 egg
4 tablespoons vegetable oil
2 tablespoons molasses or honey
½ cup water

- ❖ Preheat oven to 350 degrees F.

- ❖ Mix flour and oats. Whisk together apple, egg, oil and molasses or honey, and water. Incorporate the dry ingredients into the wet and mix into a firm dough.

- ❖ Roll dough to ¼-inch thick and cut into desired shapes.

- ❖ Bake for 30-35 minutes. Store in airtight container for up to two weeks.

Contributor's Note: My dogs love these treats and they smell so good while baking. Our furkids: Artie and Kouga.

The best thing about a man is his dog.
~ French Proverb

PB Carob Chip Cookies
Contributed by Katie

1 ¼ cups whole wheat flour
1 egg
⅜ cup milk
½ cup shortening
½ cup peanut butter
¼ cup carob chips

Unlike chocolate, carob is safe for dogs to eat. Chocolate is toxic to dogs.

❖ Preheat oven to 350 degrees F.

❖ Mix all ingredients together. Shape into walnut-sized balls, place on ungreased cookie sheet, and flatten slightly with a fork.

❖ Bake for 20 minutes. Let cool completely before feeding to your dogs.

Contributor's Note: My dog Roxy loves chocolate and peanut butter so I had to come up with a recipe so she could have her fix and me not having to worry about her getting sick.

Cheese Dog Cookies
Contributed by Julie McDonough

1 ½ cups whole wheat flour
1 ¼ cups grated cheddar cheese
¼ pound margarine
Milk as needed

❖ Preheat oven to 375 degrees F.

❖ Cream the cheese with the softened margarine and flour. Add enough milk to form into a ball. Chill for ½ hour.

Did You Know?

Try a low-fat cheese if your dog has had digestive problems when eating cheese.

❖ Roll onto floured board. Cut into shapes.

❖ Bake for 15 minutes or until slightly brown, and firm.

Makes 2 to 3 dozen, depending on size.

Contributor's Note: Daisy likes cheese, and scarfs these down.

If you don't own a dog, at least one, there is not necessarily anything wrong with you, but there may be something wrong with your life. ~ Roger Caras

Pugtastic PB & Oatmeal Cookies
Contributed by Heather Bridson

2 cups all-purpose flour
1 cup rolled oats
1 cup hot water
⅓ cup crunchy peanut butter

❖ Preheat oven to 350 degrees F.

❖ Mix dry ingredients. In a separate bowl, mix peanut butter and hot water. Combine dry and wet ingredients, knead dough, roll into walnut-sized balls and place on lightly greased cookie sheet, or I like to use parchment paper. Flatten with fork.

❖ Bake for 36-40 minutes. Cool well; will be crunchy when cooled.

Contributor's Note: I have two pugs, Vinnie and Rosie. Vinnie has a hard time with a lot of treats since he was exposed to Parvo as a puppy before we adopted him. His tummy is really touchy, but he loves his cookies! These are easy on his tummy, and I know what is in them.

A good dog deserves a good bone. ~ Ben Jonson

Oatmeal Whole Wheat Dog Cookies
Contributed by Murphy's Momma

1 cup uncooked old-fashioned oats
1 tablespoon (or 2 cubes) bouillon granules (beef, chicken or vegetable)
¾ cup non-fat dry powdered milk
1 egg-beaten
⅓ cup margarine or butter
1 ½ cups hot water
¾ cup cornmeal
3 cups whole wheat flour

❖ Preheat oven to 325 degrees F.

❖ In large bowl, pour hot water over oatmeal, margarine and bouillon granules. Let stand 5 minutes. Stir in powdered milk, cornmeal and egg. Mix well. Add flour ½ cup at a time, mixing well after each addition. I use my electric mixer until it's too stiff then mix with hands.

❖ Knead for 3-4 minutes adding more flour if necessary to make a very stiff dough. Roll out to ¼- or ½-inch thick. Cut with cookie cutters. I use bones and cat shapes for fun but you could just roll into little balls and smash with a glass if you want.

❖ Bake for 50 minutes. I use parchment paper on my cookie sheets but it's not necessary. Allow to cool and dry out until hard. Makes about 1¾ pounds. Store in airtight container.

Contributor's Note: Murphy says these are Woofing good! These cookies earned a four paw rating with our neighborhood four-leggers, too! I made these cookies using a ribbon shaped cookie cutter and sold them to raise money for our Relay for Life Cancer Walk. Raised $200 in two weeks!

The best way to get a puppy is to beg for a baby brother—and they'll settle for a puppy every time. ~ Winston Pendelton

Peanut Butter Doggy Treats
Contributed by Heather

2 cups brown rice flour
¼ cup plain oats
1 egg
1 teaspoon baking soda
2 teaspoons honey
2-3 tablespoons peanut butter
¾ cup water or more

❖ Preheat oven to 375 degrees F.

❖ Mix all ingredients together, adding water as needed to make a workable dough

❖ Roll the dough out, using the rice flour, to keep it from sticking. You will roll it out in the same way you would roll out cookies. Roll into a thickness suitable for your dog.

❖ Cut out with cookie cutters and place on greased cookie sheet or a cookie sheet lined with parchment paper if you don't want to grease the sheet.

❖ Bake for 8 minutes for thin cookies or longer if you have thick cookies.

Contributor's Note: My dogs LOVE peanut butter; the honey adds a bit of sweetness without adding a lot of sugar. The treats are wheat free for those dogs with allergies and a good alternative to boxed treats.

The biggest dog has been a pup.
~ Joaquin Miller

Best Friend Doggie Biscuits
Contributed by Amy Orvin

*1 cup cornmeal
2 cups all-purpose
flour
1 teaspoon salt
1 egg
3 tablespoons
vegetable oil
½ cup chicken broth
2 teaspoons chopped
fresh parsley*

❖ Preheat oven
to 400 degrees F. Grease 1 cookie sheet.

❖ In a large bowl, combine cornmeal, flour, and salt. In a
separate bowl, beat the egg together with the oil.

❖ Stir in chicken broth and parsley. Gradually add egg mixture
to flour mixture, stirring to combine and make a soft dough.

❖ Working on a lightly floured surface, lightly knead dough.
Roll out to a thickness of ½-inch. Cut into desired shapes
with cookie cutters. Place cookies one inch apart on the
prepared cookie sheet.

❖ Bake in preheated oven for 15 minutes or until firm.

*Contributor's Note: My two dogs love Best Friend Doggie Biscuits.
They are easy to make and the doggies get so excited when I get the
stuff out to make them.*

Minty Fresh Doggie Cookies
Contributed by Murphy's Momma

1 tablespoon vegetable oil
1 cup water
2 ½ cups whole wheat flour
½ cup oatmeal
2 tablespoons dried mint
⅓ cup chopped parsley

❖ Preheat oven to 350 degrees F.

❖ Mix oil and water. Slowly add flour and other ingredients, mix well. Roll dough out on a flat surface. Cut with bone-shaped cookie cutter and place on greased (or parchment-lined) cookie sheet. Bake for 35 minutes. Yield: 2 dozen.

Contributor's Note: If I don't want to take the time to roll them out and use cookie cutters, I will roll the dough into a log, cover with plastic wrap and put in the freezer for about 15 minutes. Then I slice and bake them. Slicing or rolling thin is the key!!!

No act of kindness, no matter how small, is ever wasted. ~ Aesop

Parmesan Herb Treats
Contributed by Barbara

1 package dry yeast
¼ cup water
2 cups chicken stock
2 tablespoons olive oil
½ cup Parmesan cheese
½ cup milk
2 tablespoons dried parsley
1 teaspoon oregano
2 teaspoons dried minced garlic
1 cup whole wheat flour
½ cup rye flour
½ cup rice flour
1 cup cracked wheat

Did You Know?

Be sure to keep all uncooked yeast dough AWAY from your dog; it can be very dangerous if ingested.

❖ Preheat oven to 325 degrees F.

❖ Dissolve yeast in water. Add stock, oil, cheese, dry milk, and herbs. Gradually blend in the flours and cracked wheat. Add enough wheat flour to form a stiff dough.

❖ Transfer to a floured surface and knead until smooth. Shape the dough into a ball and roll to ½-inch thick. Cut out treats. Place on ungreased baking sheets, spacing them about ¼-inch (6 mm) apart. Gather up the scraps, roll out again, and cut additional biscuits.

❖ Bake for 60 minutes. Remove from oven. Let cool overnight.

PB & Applesauce Dog Biscuits
Contributed by DogTipper.com

3 cups whole wheat flour
2 cups oats
1 cup peanut butter
1 cup unsweetened applesauce
1 teaspoon baking powder

❖ Preheat oven to 350 degrees F and grease two cookie sheets.

❖ Mix all ingredients, stirring until well-mixed and ready for kneading. Knead the dough on a lightly floured surface. Depending on the oil in your peanut butter, you might have to add a teaspoon of olive oil if you find the mixture is a little too crumbly.

❖ Roll the dough out to about ¼-inch thickness then cut the dough in desired shapes and place on your cookie sheets.

❖ Bake in preheated oven for about 25 minutes until lightly browned.

❖ Let the doggie biscuits cool completely before serving them to your dog or refrigerating them.

Avoid Chocolate!

Chocolates and canines don't mix! Chocolate contains two active ingredients, caffeine and theobromine, both of which can make your dog sick.

The initial signs of chocolate toxicity are vomiting and diarrhea. Your dog will breathe quickly, and his heart will race. If he has eaten a high enough dose of chocolate, he will start convulsing, and he may die.

So, how much is too much? Dark cooking chocolate has more toxic ingredients than either milk chocolate or white chocolate, and unsweetened baking chocolate has most of all. Eight ounces of milk chocolate is enough to potentially kill a 10-pound dog.

If you suspect your dog has stolen some chocolate, give your veterinarian a call with information on your dog's body weight, the quantity of chocolate that is missing, and what type of chocolate it is. She will be able to work out how much caffeine and theobromine has been eaten, and whether or not your dog is likely to become sick. Treatment is basically supportive until your dog recovers with intravenous fluids, activated charcoal and muscle relaxants to control any tremors or seizures.

PB & Pumpkin Dog Treats
Contributed by Allison L.

2 ½ cups whole wheat flour
2 eggs
½ cup canned pumpkin
2 tablespoons peanut butter
¼ cup dried cranberries
½ teaspoon salt
½ teaspoon ground cinnamon
⅓ cup rolled oats (not instant)

❖ Preheat oven to 350 degrees F.

❖ Whisk together the flour, eggs, pumpkin, peanut butter, salt, oats, dried cranberries and cinnamon in a bowl. Add water as needed to help make the dough workable, but the dough should be dry and stiff.

❖ Roll the dough into a ½-inch-thick roll. Cut into ½-inch pieces.

❖ Bake until hard, about 40 minutes.

Contributor's Note: I got part of this recipe online a while back and just tweaked it to my dog's liking and to make it my own.

If a dog will not come to you after having looked you in the face, you should go home and examine your conscience. ~ Woodrow Wilson

Carrot & Cheese Biscuits
Contributed by DogTipper.com

2 ¾ cups whole wheat flour
1 cup shredded carrots
1 cup shredded cheese
2 cup bran cereal, crushed (do NOT use raisin bran)
2 tablespoons olive oil
2 teaspoons baking powder
1 ½ cups water

❖ Preheat oven to 350 degrees F. Grease baking sheets.

❖ Mix carrots, cheese and oil in a large bowl; in a smaller bowl, mix dry ingredients.

❖ Add the dry ingredients to the carrot-cheese-oil mixture then add water, mixing well.

❖ Pinch off a ping pong ball-sized piece of dough, drop onto cookie sheet, and slightly flatten with a fork.

❖ Bake for 25 minutes until browned. Cool and store.

Everyday Biscuits
Contributed by Amy Orvin

2 teaspoons dry yeast
½ cup lukewarm
water
2 tablespoons dry
parsley
2 tablespoons minced
garlic
1 ½ cups chicken
broth
3 tablespoons honey
1 egg
5-6 cups whole wheat
flour

- ❖ Preheat oven to 350 degrees F.

- ❖ In a large bowl, dissolve yeast in warm water. Stir in the parsley, garlic, broth, honey, and egg. Gradually blend in flour, adding enough to form a stiff dough.

- ❖ Transfer to a floured surface and knead until smooth (about 3-5 minutes). Shape dough into a ball, and roll to ¼-inch (6 mm) thick. Using small bone-shaped cookie cutters, make biscuits! Transfer to ungreased baking sheets, spacing them about ¼-inch (6 mm) apart. Gather scraps, roll out again, and cut additional biscuits.

- ❖ Bake for 30 minutes. Remove from oven and turn over. Bake for an additional 15 minutes, or until lightly browned on both sides. Let cool overnight.

Contributor's Note: I have two dogs, Toby and Sushi, and they are my babies.

Easy Microwave Dog Cookies
Contributed by Murphy's Momma

1 cup whole-wheat flour
¾ cup dry milk
¼ cup cornmeal
⅓ cup shortening
1 tablespoon bouillon granules
½ cup regular flour
½ cup quick cooking oats
1 teaspoon sugar
1 egg slightly beaten
½ cup hot water

❖ Mix all together, using hands if necessary. Roll out and cut into shapes. Cook in microwave at 50 percent power for 5+ minutes, rotating plate. Watch closely; they burn easy when they are rolled thin.

Contributor's Note: Tips: I used part rye, whole-wheat flour and wheat germ in place of the cup of plain whole-wheat flour. Also used long cooking/old fashioned oats instead of quick cooking and they turned out fine. I rolled the dough thin then used a shot glass to cut out small cookies. I "baked" them on paper plates and noticed that, depending on the power of your microwave, they do burn quickly so keep a close eye on them.

Next time I will try substituting peanut butter for the shortening. I also always keep all homemade dog cookies in the freezer since there are no preservatives. Plus, my dogs love a cold cookie! These sure are a hit with all my four-legged friends!

Peanut Butter Bones
Contributed by DogTipper.com

1 cup peanut butter (creamy or crunchy)
1 cup whole wheat flour
1 cup all-purpose flour
2 tablespoons olive oil
1 cup multigrain cereal or bran flakes, crushed (do NOT use cereals with raisins)
½ cup shredded carrots
2 tablespoons baking powder
1 tablespoon molasses
½ cup water

- ❖ Preheat oven to 350 degrees F.

- ❖ Mix dry ingredients then add wet ingredients, adding water a little at a time. The amount of water you'll need will vary based on the oil in the peanut butter.

- ❖ Work the dough on a lightly floured surface. Roll out to about a ¼-inch thickness then cut with a cookie cutter.

- ❖ After you cut out the bones, bring together the scraps, knead the dough, and continue cutting until you've used up all the dough. Place the bones on a greased or parchment-lined cookie sheet.

- ❖ Bake in preheated oven: After baking the bones until browned on both sides, remove from the oven, set them out and let them cool completely to make them crisper.

The dog was created specially for children. He is the god of frolic. ~ Henry Ward Beecher

Anise Seed Dog Treats
Contributed by DogTipper.com

2 cups all-purpose flour
¼ cup butter softened to room
temperature
¼ cup molasses
1 egg
2 teaspoons anise seed
1 teaspoon baking powder

Did You Know?

Some dogs react to anise like cats to catnip. Try a sprinkle in a favorite plush toy!

❖ Preheat oven to 350 degrees F and grease two cookie sheets.

❖ Mix all the ingredients together; the result is a heavy, slightly sticky dough.

❖ Pinch small pieces about the size of a large marble, roll between your palms and slightly flattened with a fork before putting it on the cookie sheet.

❖ Bake in the preheated oven; these cook quickly so they'll be ready in about 15 minutes. Let them cool completely before refrigerating (and your kitchen will smell wonderful in the meantime!)

My best friend is the one who brings out the best in me. ~ Henry Ford

Yummy Dog Biscuits
Contributed by Julie McDonough

2 ½ cups whole wheat flour
½ cup milk
1 teaspoon garlic powder
1 large egg, beaten
2 tablespoons flavoring
(bacon drippings, chicken or
beef stock — your choice)

❖ Preheat the oven to 350 degrees F and lightly spray or grease a cookie sheet.

❖ Lightly flour a surface to roll the dough on. In a medium bowl, mix dry ingredients. Add the flavoring you selected and the beaten egg to the bowl and mix well. Note: This is a pretty stiff dough. If you find it to be too stiff to work with, just add a touch more of the chicken stock (or whatever else you're using).

❖ Roll out the dough to about a ¼-inch thickness. Use a pizza cutter or a few different, bone-shaped cookie cutters to cut the dough into the desired size.

❖ Bake for 30 minutes and let cool before treating your happy dog to his or her new favorite biscuit recipe!

Contributor's Note: My dog Daisy loves these!

Chicken & Cheese Biscuits
Contributed by DogTipper.com

*1 ½ cups shredded, cooked
chicken
¾ cup chicken broth, divided
½ cup shredded cheese
1 cup whole wheat flour
1 cup all-purpose flour*

Did You Know?

**The easiest way to
shred cooked chicken
is with two forks.**

❖ Preheat oven to 350
degrees F and grease two
cookie sheets.

❖ Toss chicken and ½-cup chicken broth in a blender or food
processor and mix until it's the consistency of baby food.

❖ In a separate bowl, mix flours and cheese then add
chicken/chicken broth mixture. As you mix, slowly add a
teaspoon of reserved broth at a time until the dough is the
right consistency to knead. The dough should be heavy but
shouldn't be too dry (you need more broth) or too sticky (you
need more flour).

❖ Knead the dough on a lightly floured surface and roll it to
about ¼-inch thickness. Cut with cookie cutters then place on
sheet.

❖ Bake for half an hour then remove from oven and allow the
treats to cool completely before refrigerating.

Pear & Molasses Dog Biscuits
Contributed by DogTipper.com

2 cups chopped pears, cored
2 ½ cups whole wheat flour
¼ cup water
1 tablespoon baking powder
3 tablespoons molasses

❖ Preheat oven to 350 degrees F and grease a cookie sheet.

❖ Mix all ingredients in a large bowl. The result is a very sticky, heavy dough. Turn out the dough on a lightly floured surface then knead. Roll it out to about ¼-inch thickness then cut it in squares. Place the biscuits on a greased (or parchment-lined) cookie sheet.

❖ Bake for half an hour (the bottom of the biscuits should be golden brown when done) then cool the biscuits completely before refrigerating or serving.

Did You Know?

Dogs can NOT eat pear pips or seeds. Like apple seeds, cherry pips, peach pits, plum pips, and apricot pips, these seeds contain a compound that breaks down into cyanide. Toss them in the trash!

Oatmeal-Turkey Dog Biscuits
Contributed by DogTipper.com

1 ¾ cups whole wheat flour
2 ½ cups quick cooking oats
1 teaspoon baking powder
1 cup turkey (or chicken) broth
1 ½ cups shredded turkey (or chicken)

❖ Preheat the oven to 350 degrees F, and grease cookie sheets.

❖ Mix dry ingredients in a large bowl and set aside. In your blender, add broth and turkey then blend to the consistency of baby food. Add this meat mixture to the dry ingredients and mix well.

❖ Turn out the dough on a lightly floured surface and knead. This is a heavy dough so it takes some muscle! Roll out the dough and cut into shapes; place on greased (or parchment-lined) cookie sheets.

❖ Bake for about 25 minutes until the treats are golden brown.

❖ Be sure to cool the biscuits completely before serving to your dog or refrigerating. Our dogs loved these!

If you pick up a starving dog and make him prosperous, he will not bite you; that is the principal difference between a dog and a man. ~ Mark Twain

Saving on Fruit & Vegetable Purchases

The most economical time to buy fruits and vegetables for your dog treats is when they're in season; you can process and freeze most for use later in the year.

Here's a look at some of the season's best buys:

Fall: Acorn squash, Apples (discard seeds), Butternut Squash, Figs, Pears, Pumpkin, Sweet Potatoes

Winter: Radishes, Rutabagas, Turnips

Spring: Apricots, Carrots, Mango, Spinach, Strawberries, Snow Peas, Sugar Snap Peas

Summer: Blackberries, Blueberries, Green Beans, Peaches, Plums, Raspberries, Watermelon, Zucchini

Fishy Fido Treats

Fishy Brownies
Contributed by Kelli

2 cans tuna
2 eggs
1½ cups all-purpose flour
2 tablespoons Parmesan cheese
Garlic powder, to taste

- ❖ Preheat oven to 350 degrees F.

- ❖ Mix all ingredients and transfer mix into a greased 9" x 9" or similar baking pan. Bake for about 30 minutes.

- ❖ Check treats about half way through baking time so they do not burn. Cut into any size pieces you wish.

Contributor's Note: My dogs go nuts for the recipe, especially for agility training. I'm sure they would do anything for a bite!

Friendship is the only cement that will hold the world together. ~ Woodrow Wilson

Super Tuna Treaties
Contributed by Carolsue

1 can (12-ounce) tuna, undrained
2 eggs
1½ cups flour (whole wheat,
preferably)
¼ cup Parmesan cheese

> ### Did You Know?
>
> **If you don't have a 9" x 13" pan, you can substitute two 8" square pans.**

❖ Preheat oven to 350 degrees F.

❖ Mix ingredients and press into a greased 9" x13" pan. Mixture will be stiff.

❖ Bake for 20 minutes.

❖ After cooling, cut into strips then dice strips into small cubes.

❖ Refrigerate or freeze.

Contributor's Note: My dog's name is Spooky. She's an 11-year-old German Short Haired Pointer that I got from the pound.

No man can be condemned for owning a dog. As long as he has a dog, he has a friend; and the poorer he gets, the better friend he has. ~ Will Rogers

Holy Mackerel
Contributed by Kirby the Dorkie,
www.kirbythedorkie.com

1 can (15-ounce) mackerel
1½ cups instant mashed potatoes
2 eggs, beaten
1 tablespoon lemon juice
2 tablespoon chopped parsley
¼ teaspoon sea salt *

- ❖ Preheat oven to 350 degrees F.

- ❖ Drain mackerel, reserving the juice. Break apart and carefully remove the spine bones.

- ❖ In a medium bowl, thoroughly mix together all of the ingredients. Add just enough of the mackerel juice to help the ingredients stick together. (Fish oils are very good for the skin but I also added a tablespoon of flax meal since Kirby has such dry skin - actually I add flax meal to almost everything he eats.)

- ❖ Shape into small balls or patties, if preferred. The dryness causes them to be a little hard to form but they will bake to a perfect crunchy on the outside, soft on the inside morsel.

- ❖ Arrange on a parchment-lined or greased cookie sheet. Bake for 20 minutes. Cool and serve. These will keep in the refrigerator for up to a week or can be frozen for at least a month.

* Contributor's Note: Sea salt (not table salt) is considered healthy and acceptable for dogs but can be omitted.

Contributor's Note: Blog: www.kirbythedorkie.com about a little dog with a big heart. I am particular about everything Kirby eats and any products that he comes into contact with. He is probably one of the healthiest, green dogs around.

I've seen a look in dogs' eyes, a quickly vanishing look of amazing contempt, and I am convinced that dogs think humans are nuts. ~ John Steinbeck

Creamy Fish
Contributed by Nancy

We are fishermen, so we have a lot of fish dinners. When there is left over fish, we mix it with enough plain or vanilla-flavored yogurt to make a little soup.

We then freeze it in small ice cube trays. It makes a great quick, easy and cool treats for dogs on the go.

Contributor's Note: We have friends that do this with canned tuna.

The average dog is a nicer person than the average person. ~ Andy Rooney

Sardine Delights
Contributed by cstironkat

3½ cans sardines
¼ cup milk powder
¼ cup wheat germ

- ❖ Preheat oven 350 degrees F. Line a cookie sheet with foil or parchment paper.

- ❖ Combine all ingredients and mix well. Roll mixture into balls and flatten with a fork. Bake 15 minutes.

- ❖ Store in refrigerator or freeze.

Contributor's Note: Cats love this recipe, too.

Animals are such agreeable friends—they ask no questions; they pass no criticisms. ~ George Eliot

Tasty Tuna Treats
Contributed by Kirby the Dorkie,
www.kirbythedorkie.com

2 (5-ounce) cans tuna
1 tablespoon salmon oil*
1 ½ cups organic spelt
flour**
½ cup Parmesan cheese
1 egg
½ cup water

- ❖ Preheat oven to 350 degrees F.

- ❖ Drain tuna, saving the liquid. Puree tuna with oil. Take the saved liquid and add enough water to make ½ cup.

- ❖ Thoroughly combine all ingredients in a medium-sized bowl. Using a spatula, spread mixture on a greased or parchment-lined jellyroll pan. (If you really want to cut cookie shapes then you can reduce or omit the water or add more flour until you have a better consistency to work with.)

- ❖ Bake for 20 minutes. Turn off the oven and let sit for another 20 minutes with the door slightly ajar. Remove to cutting board. Slice into small pieces using pizza cutter. These can keep in an airtight container in the refrigerator for several weeks.

You can substitute light olive oil or canola oil.
**You can use brown rice flour or whole wheat flour. Spelt is naturally high in fiber, contains significantly more protein than wheat, is also higher in B complex vitamins, and both simple and complex carbohydrates. Another important benefit is that some gluten-sensitive people have been able to include spelt-based foods in their diets.*

Training Treats

Liver Treats
Contributed by Lin

Lin notes, "Freeze-dried liver treats are very expensive. These are fresher and inexpensive enough to use for training and treats."

1 pound beef liver (as thinly cut as you can find)

- ❖ Preheat oven to 400 degrees F.

- ❖ Slice liver into small pieces. Place on cookie sheet.

- ❖ Bake for 15-20 minutes until cooked, dried, and crispy.

- ❖ Freeze in vacuum bags.

Contributor's Note: Blossom is a 5-year-old Parson Russell Terrier. She has changed my life by "encouraging" me to exercise with her...we bike and walk alternately every day of the week! Also, we are into agility and attend training at a local dog training center.

Some dogs have difficulties with garlic, even in moderation. Check with your vet before adding new ingredients to your dog's treats and diet.

To his dog, every man is Napoleon; hence the constant popularity of dogs. ~ Aldous Huxley

Liver Brownies
Contributed by cstironkat

1 pound beef liver
3 tablespoons peanut butter
2 cups whole wheat flour
1 cup rice, barley, or carrots

❖ Preheat oven to 350 degrees F.

❖ Cook rice or barley according to directions (carrots can be left raw).

❖ Puree liver in food processor and mix with the peanut butter. In separate bowl, mix flour and barley, rice or carrots. Add liver mixture.

❖ Pour into 9x9 inch pan and bake for 20 minutes.

❖ Let cool, cut into pieces and store in refrigerator for up to one week.

Contributor's Note: My rescued dogs Kouga and Artie love these brownies.

The reason dogs have so many friends is because they wag their tails instead of their tongues. ~ Unknown

Garlic Hot Dog Training Treats
Contributed by Kelli

2 hot dogs cut into bite-sized chunks
Garlic powder

- ❖ Cut hot dogs into bite-sized pieces according to your dog's size.

- ❖ Lay hot dogs on a microwavable plate and sprinkle a thin layer of garlic powder over them.

- ❖ Microwave for about 2 minutes or until the hot dogs have dried out a bit (they will be a little greasy).

- ❖ Let the hot dogs cool on a paper towel to soak up excess grease.

- ❖ Keep refrigerated. Freeze for longer storage.

Contributor's Note: My Cattle Dog goes nuts for these treats at agility class! She would do a course a thousand times over just for one piece of delicious hot dog, I'm sure!

If dogs could talk it would take a lot of the fun out of owning one. ~ Andy Rooney

Crazeedog Training Treats
Contributed by Crazeedogs

2 cups salmon
2-3 eggs
2-3 cups whole wheat flour
2 tablespoons natural applesauce
1 tablespoon local honey

❖ Preheat oven to 375 degrees F.

❖ Mix all ingredients together, you may need to adjust flour or add an egg if mixture is too dry or wet. Mixture should be a thick, moist consistency.

❖ Grease large cookie sheet and spread mixture. I sprinkle with parsley and garlic powder for extra flavor. Cook at 375 degrees for 20 minutes. Adjust cooking time for your oven.

❖ Let cool 10 minutes and slice in bite size pieces or break apart with hands and store in baggies to freeze. You can break off pieces as needed for training. Even picky pups love these soft treats. Have fun training your pups!

Contributor's Note: I have seven dogs and needed an inexpensive way to make treats for our agility, obedience and trick training. This recipe is great in that you can easily add and adjust items to your personal preferences. My favorite rescue is the Humane Society of Columbiana County. We adopted our Cubby there and the folks are so loving and take such great care of all the animals. All of the animals are saved from abuse and neglect situations. The best part about this recipe is its versatility in that you can make them pretty much any flavor! I have made them in Liver, Salmon, Chicken, Sardine and even Pumpkin or Sweet Potato etc.

Venison Cookies
Contributed by Kelli

2 cups pureed venison
2 carrots, minced
5 tablespoons olive oil
4 tablespoons honey
½ cup milk
2 eggs
¼ cup chopped parsley
2 teaspoons baking soda
½ cup milled flax
½ cup cracked wheat
4 cups brown rice flour

❖ Preheat oven to 350 degrees F. Mix all ingredients in a large bowl until dough forms, add more flour if needed. Knead and roll into onto 2 parchment-covered cookie sheets. Score to preferred size with pizza cutter or knife. Bake for 20 minutes.

❖ Reduce heat to 300 degrees F and return to oven until dried and hardened (about 1½ hours). Scored treats should easily break into pieces after cooled.

Contributor's Note: My three terriers love venison, and we do lots of training! So I make these treats often and cut them into tiny squares for training tidbits.

Don't walk in front of me,
I may not follow.
Don't walk behind me,
I may not lead. Walk
Beside me and be my friend.
~ Albert Camus

Liver Training Treats
Contributed by DogTipper.com

1 pound raw liver, rinsed
2 cups whole wheat flour
1 egg
½ cup water

- ❖ Preheat oven to 350 degrees F.

- ❖ Rinse liver with cold water then toss liver into the blender or food processor. Blend to malt consistency.

- ❖ In a mixing bowl, pour the liver and mix with flour, egg and water. Stir well. The result is a heavy batter. Pour the batter onto a well-greased cookie sheet (one with a good lip). This mix won't rise much at all.

- ❖ Bake for 30 minutes. Take the cookie sheet out and score the treats into ½ -inch squares.

- ❖ Turn off your oven and return the cookie sheet with the scored treats back to the oven for about 10 minutes to dry out the treats. After 10 minutes, turn off oven, flip treats again and return the cookie sheet to the oven and leave it there until the oven cools.

When you take the treats out of the oven, if they're not completely cooled, let them cool on the counter before you finally bag them up and refrigerate them.

You do not own a dog, the dog owns you. ~ Unknown

Hot Dog Training Treats
Contributed by DogTipper.com

1 package hot dogs (preferably organic)

❖ Cut hot dogs into about ¼-inch slices. Put hot dog medallions on 6 layers of paper towels.

> **To remove some of the salt in hot dogs, soak the wieners in cool water overnight in the refrigerator.**

❖ Pop everything (including paper towels) in microwave and cook for 5 minutes. At the end of time, you should see plenty of grease on the paper towels; take another paper towel and blot grease off top of the hot dogs.

❖ *Note:* Microwave times will vary. When some treats begin to darken around the edges, they're done.

There is no psychiatrist in the world like a puppy licking your face. ~ Bern Williams

Choosing Training Treats

We love using training treats with our dogs; both Irie and Tiki have learned extremely quickly thanks to positive reinforcement training.

Remember that you'll need MANY training treats when initially training your dog so the key is first to make training treats small (think pea-sized) and compensate by reducing your dog's meal size as well.

Meat treats work best with many dogs and often the stronger-scented treats like liver are the most effective. Allowing refrigerated treats to warm to room temperature before you use them will bring out the scent to further entice your dog.

You'll also get better results if training treats are used exclusively for training. (You can prepare other treats for everyday use.) If you reserve these high-value treats for training sessions, you'll see the greatest response.

Savory Meat Treats

Schooner's Spinach Snacks
Contributed by S. Gilbert
Recipe by Kol's Notes, kolchakpuggle.com

Contributor's Note: This is a recipe that Jodi from Kol's Notes (kolchakpuggle.com) came up with for Schooner because Schooner hates vegetables. I had tried some of her recipes with vegetables, and they were a no-go with Schooner. (Skipper loves vegetables.) I made Spinach Treats for Schooner and to my surprise he loves them. Seriously, these treats are so woofing easy to make, plus they are good for you. Didn't your Mama always tell you to eat your spinach?

1 cup extra lean ground chicken
2 cups cooked spinach, drained (we used frozen)
1 egg white
1 teaspoon
mixed Italian seasonings like oregano, sage or thyme

- ❖ Preheat oven to 350 degrees F.

- ❖ Use your hands to squeeze any excess moisture out of the spinach. In a large bowl, combine chicken, spinach, egg white and seasonings. Mix well.

- ❖ Spoon bite-sized pieces onto a parchment-lined cookie sheet. Our mini melon ball scoop was exactly the perfect size to scoop with.

- ❖ Place in the oven and bake for 45 minutes. Turn oven down to 200 degrees F and allow treats to dry for 2 - 3 hours. Alternatively, you could make these in the dehydrator.

Mysterious Meatballs
Contributed by Robin Trelz

1 pound ground chuck
½ cup uncooked minute rice
1 egg (beaten)
2 tablespoons ketchup
¼ cup plain breadcrumbs
Grated Parmesan cheese

❖ Preheat oven to 350 degrees F.

❖ Mix all ingredients together except cheese. Make small bite sized meatballs (I use a melon scooper). Place meatballs in a 9" x 12" baking dish sprayed with baking spray. Sprinkle with Parmesan cheese. Bake 35-45 minutes until thoroughly cooked and golden brown.

❖ These keep for up to three days in the refrigerator for GREAT treats! I make a lot at once and freeze them and thaw as needed.

Contributor's Note: My dogs love these treats! They are very nice bite-sized treats. I bake a lot for my dogs but these are truly their very favorite treat!

Meaty Bone Cookies
Contributed by Shaker Dog Lover

2 cups flour (preferably organic and multigrain)
2 tablespoons oil
½ cup ground beef or chicken liver
½ cup water

- ❖ Preheat oven to 350 degrees F.

- ❖ Combine all the ingredients and mix until smooth (you can also use a food processor).

- ❖ With a rolling pin on a floured surface, roll dough to ⅓ inch thick then cut with favorite cookie cutter.

- ❖ Bake for 40 minutes or until browned. Let them stand on the counter to dry a little before storing.

Contributor's Note: This is a recipe and cookies that I have been making for my friends' dogs for their birthday parties and also Christmas!

Every dog must have his day.
~ Jonathan Swift

Doggy Meatloaf
Contributed by Letessha Williams

½ pound ground beef
2 teaspoons bread crumbs
2 teaspoons water

❖ Preheat oven to 350 degrees F.

❖ Roll meat into a loaf and bake for 60 minutes.

Contributor's Note: My dog is a Chihuahua, and she loves this recipe.

Did You Know?

Any time you're working with meatloaf, if you lightly oil your hands, the meat won't stick to your fingers.

Dogs never lie about love.
~ Jeffrey Moussaieff Masson

Meatball Treat Balls
Contributed by Heather Carter

5 pounds ground beef
3 cups oatmeal
1 cup molasses
½ cup wheat germ
10 eggs
2 packets unflavored gelatin

Did You Know?

Wheat germ is often cited as a way to support good skin and coat quality.

❖ Mix together with
  your hands. Then form into ½-inch balls, depending on the
  size of your dog.

❖ Fry several at a time in a pan on medium high until
  thoroughly cooked. We put ours into a freezer bag and keep
  them in the bottom of the fridge and give 1 or 2 daily. My
  dogs DROOL over this treat!

*Contributor's Note: I have two dogs, a 10-year-old German
Shepherd named Midnight who we've had since she was 9 weeks old
and our newest addition to the house, Sasha, an 11-week-old
German Shepherd we rescued from a shelter just two weeks ago!*

*You think those dogs will not be in heaven! I tell you
they will be there long before any of us. ~ Robert
Louis Stevenson*

Liver Cornbread
Contributed by DogTipper.com

1 small box cornbread mix
1 egg
1 pound liver, rinsed

- ❖ Preheat oven to 350 degrees F.

- ❖ In a blender, blend liver to a malt consistency. Pour liver in a mixing bowl, add cornbread mix, and one egg. Stir.

- ❖ Pour batter onto well-greased or parchment-lined cookie sheet (with a ½-inch raised edge).

- ❖ Bake for 30 minutes. Cool then refrigerate.

The Liver Cornbread is a real favorite with our dogs; it's a lighter consistency than the Liver Training Treats so it doesn't work out as well for putting in your pocket or treat bag to use during training; it's best as an after-walk treat.

Chicken Liver Squares
Contributed by DogTipper.com

1 pound chicken livers
1 pound chicken
3 eggs

❖ Preheat oven to 220 degrees F. Line two cookie sheets with parchment paper or lightly grease cookie sheets.

❖ Add chicken and eggs to blender or food processor and chop then mix. Add chicken livers to mixture, pouring entire container of livers, juices and all, into mixture. Mix until you have a malt-like consistency.

❖ Pour the mixture in the center of the two cookie sheets then bake. After one hour, cut each mixture into one-inch squares and flip so that all sides of the treats will brown. Bake for one more hour.

❖ When treats are browned, turn off the oven but leave the cookie sheets in the heated oven to cool for several hours. Cool treats completely before serving or refrigerating. Refrigerate or freeze all treats; they'll last about two weeks in the refrigerator.

When a man's dog turns against him, it is time for his wife to pack her trunk and go home to mamma. ~ Mark Twain

Stuffable Treats

No-Bake Stuffed Treats
Contributed by Zelda's Mama

3 cups rolled oats
1 cup peanut butter
½ cup milk

❖ Combine peanut butter and milk until it makes a paste.

❖ Gradually fold in oats (about ½ cup at a time). Be patient and be sure to coat oats thoroughly with peanut butter/milk mixture.

❖ Form into balls (for individual treats) or cylinder shapes (to fit in Kong). Store in refrigerator for up to 2 weeks.

Contributor's Note: Zelda's Mama adopted Zelda from the Kanawha Charleston Humane Association Shelter in Charleston, West Virginia on December 31, 2011. It's been a hopeless love story ever since. The KCHA is always looking for rescues to save as many animals as possible. Please take a look and see if you're interested in any.

Peanut & Cheese Layers
Contributed by Stephanie H

Peanut butter
Canned cheese

❖ Squirt a little cheese in the Kong, then add a layer of peanut butter, then a layer of cheese. Finish with a layer of peanut butter.

❖ Freeze the stuffed Kong overnight. Put it out in the house in the morning before you leave the doggy alone, this way he has layers of different flavors to entertain himself as the Kong thaws. Because this is frozen, he can't eat everything all at once.

Contributor's Note: This is a trick I used with a friend's dog who hated when mommy left home. I currently do not have my own dog but in the past I have fostered dogs for the Humane Society of West Texas. I have used peanut butter and meat paste with my cats. I use a puppy Kong because all animals need entertainment.

The dog is a gentleman; I hope to go to his heaven not man's. ~ Mark Twain

PB & Cream Cheese
Contributed by S. Gilbert

6 tablespoons peanut butter
3 tablespoons cream cheese

❖ Mix together. Put in a Kong or make little balls. Put in freezer until you are ready to give it to your dogs.

❖ I stuff bones from the butcher after they have eaten all the bone marrow out of the bones. Works great. I stuff the bones and put in the freezer. I freeze them because it takes them longer to get the mix out. Great when you are leaving the house. It keeps my dogs busy.

Contributor's Note: Schooner and Skipper love when I cook for them. They know when we leave the house they will get their frozen stuffed bones to keep them busy while we are gone. We have a camera so we can see what they are doing while we are gone from the house: they are busy getting the stuffing out of their bones!

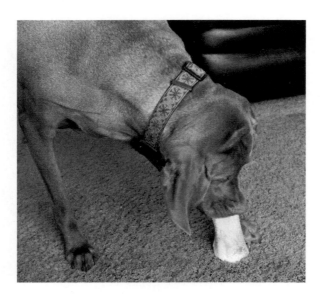

Salmon & Sweet Potato
Contributed by NancyParadise

1 salmon steak
1 sweet potato, peeled and cut into 1 ½" chunks

- ❖ I steam salmon and sweet potato and mix to a mush and stuff Kong toy.

- ❖ Great for dogs on limited ingredient diets.

Contributor's Note: My dog Reba is on a limited ingredient diet. I created this recipe to fit her needs.

Acquiring a dog may be the only opportunity a human has to choose a relative. ~ Mordecai Siegal

Stuffable Chicken & Carrots
Contributed by Jude

1 chicken breast, deboned
3 carrots, peeled and
chopped
1 cup rice

Did You Know?

Raw carrots are good snacks for dogs...and good for their teeth!

❖ I boil all the above and put in food processor.

❖ I will freeze in an ice cube tray and only thaw one 'cube' at a time. The dogs love it!

Contributor's Note: I have three Papillons who all have very sensitive stomachs. They cannot eat commercial treats due to all the additives. The stuffable chicken and carrots are a wonderful healthy treat.

Until one has loved an animal, a part of one's soul remains unawakened. ~ Anatole France

Picky Dog PB & Pumpkin
Contributed by Cathy

¼ cup smooth peanut butter
⅛ cup pure pumpkin (not pie filling)

❖ Mix peanut butter and pumpkin, by hand, until mixed well.

❖ Refrigerate for 15 minutes. Spoon mixture into Kong toys.

❖ Recipe will need to be adjusted for very large Kongs. You can also fill Kongs right after mixing ingredients - then place Kongs in freezer until mixture is frozen solid for a great summer treat.

Contributor's Note: I have two picky little lap dogs. This is one treat they will actually eat. It allows me to incorporate pumpkin into the treat, otherwise they will not eat pumpkin.

Honey Sweet Potato Stuffing
Contributed by Cathy

1 cooked, mashed sweet potato
1 tablespoon honey

❖ Mix ingredients together and cook in microwave until heated through. You can add a teaspoon of water if necessary, but do not make mixture too thin.

❖ Refrigerate mixture until cool and then spoon into Kong toys.

Contributor's Note: This recipe will fill several small Kongs or one large. Dogs should always be supervised, and it is good to know your dog's allergies.

Dogs are better than human beings because they know but they do not tell. ~ Emily Dickinson

Pigskin Surprise
contributed by DogTipper.com

1 cup chicharrónes or pork rinds
1 egg
2-3 soft dog treats

❖ Soft cook the egg by breaking it in a bowl, whipping lightly with a fork, and microwaving for one minute. The egg should still be slightly runny. Allow the egg to cool completely.

❖ Use a soft dog treat to plug the small hole at the end of the Kong. Other options are cheese (cream cheese works well), a bit of lunchmeat, or a small plug of soft bread.

❖ Chicharrónes, fried pork skin, are next. Stuff into Kong; about ⅓ through stuffing, add a portion of the egg. Alternate layers of pork rinds and egg until the Kong is filled.

❖ Plug the larger opening in the Kong with soft treats; if that doesn't work, top it with some cheese or peanut butter.

❖ You can make this treat ahead of time and freeze it.

Easy Banana Yogurt
Contributed by Cathy

½ cup plain yogurt
1 small jar banana baby food

❖ Mix well and carefully spoon into Kong. It can be frozen in the Kong for a great summer treat.

Contributor's Note: Know your dog's allergies. Stuffed Kongs are messy – best if fed outdoors. Enjoy!

Money will buy you a pretty good dog, but it won't buy the wag of his tail. ~ Henry Wheeler Shaw

Frozen Tuna Salad
Contributed by Amy Orvin

1 (6-ounce) can light tuna
2 tablespoons plain yogurt
¼ cup grated carrot

- ❖ Mix all ingredients.

- ❖ Spoon into Kong toy. Freeze.

Contributor's Note: My dogs love Kong toys especially the stuff that's inside the toy.

I am because my little dog knows me.
~ Gertrude Stein

Using Stuffable Treats

A stuffable toy can be a great way to keep your dog busy for a while, and it can be a great tool for preventing boredom, working through separation anxiety, and just livening up your dog's mealtime! Try:

- ❖ a combination of dry kibble and wet dog food. Mix the two or use the wet dog food as plugs at either end to hold the kibble, a fun way to feed your dog breakfast or dinner!

- ❖ vegetables like green beans and carrots. You can stuff the toy completely or use peanut butter to plug the ends.

- ❖ fruits such as diced apple and banana, perhaps with some plain cereal or some kibble. The banana is especially helpful for acting as the "glue" to hold everything together.

- ❖ frozen plain (no salt, no seasoning) chicken broth, great for a summer treat!

- ❖ scrambled eggs

- ❖ boiled chicken and mashed potatoes

Frozen Treats

Frozen Puppy Pops
Contributed by Pamela Douglas Webster, www.somethingwagging.com

1 cup plain yogurt
1 cup peanut butter
2 tablespoons honey

❖ Whip the ingredients together. Pour into ice cube trays and freeze for several hours.

❖ Pop out to serve on a hot day.

Contributor's Note: Everyone at Something Wagging This Way Comes (www.somethingwagging.com) likes puppy pops. They're even delicious to humans.

Some people talk to animals. Not many listen though. That's the problem. ~ A.A. Milne

Roastcicles
Contributed by Rick

A favorite meal around here is roast. Before everyone heads out for their busy day we place a roast, usually deer but any meat will do, in a pan with carrots, potatoes, cabbage, and mushrooms. We then fill the pan with water and slow cook it in the oven at 275 degrees. When we get home for dinner the house smells amazing. When the meal is done and it's time for cleanup, we bust out the skinny ice cube trays.

We use the skinny type so that the finished product isn't too big or hard and is less likely to hurt the doggies' teeth. We fill the trays up and freeze them. When the pups need a cool treat, there is a free delectable dish waiting for them just inside the freezer door.

Contributor's Note: There are hot days you can spot a dog staring at the refrigerator. They are asking for a roastcicle.

A dog has but one aim in life…to bestow his heart.
~ J.R. Ackerley

PB & Yogurt Pupsicles
Versions contributed by LennyG; Julie Berg; and Maureen

1 (32-ounce) container of yogurt
1 cup peanut butter

- ❖ Put the peanut butter in a microwave-safe container and microwave until melted.

- ❖ Mix the yogurt and melted peanut butter together thoroughly in a bowl.

- ❖ Pour mixture into bone-shaped ice cube trays or cupcake liners and freeze.

Contributor's Note from LennyG (and Tiki, above): Monmouth County (NJ) SPCA is the rescue organization we support.

Contributor's Note from Julie Berg: Ralphie, my beloved longhaired dachshund, absolutely goes nuts for anything peanut butter. He is even excited to take his medication because he gets a little peanut butter with it. Ralphie is also a certified therapy dog, and he gets one of these as a special treat after we get home from a therapy session.

If your dog likes peanut butter and likes frozen treats (my dogs always have) then they will love these treats! They're great for cooling off in the summer, or anytime you want to spoil your dog with some healthy peanut butter goodness!

Contributor's Note from Maureen: I have two puppies that I adore. I am a dog lover at heart, and have a line of Doggy Silhouette Necklaces in my shop, Release Me Creations (www.ReleaseMeCreations.com), where $8 from every sale goes to Paws in the City Rescue of Dallas.

The greatness of a nation and its moral progress can be judged by the way its animals are treated. ~ Mahatma Gandhi

Chilly Dog
Contributed by M.j. with versions from Heather & Maria

32 ounces plain yogurt
1 mashed ripe banana
2 tablespoons peanut butter
2 tablespoons honey

❖ Mix all of the ingredients with a blender or mixer and freeze in ice cube trays. Small paper cups and disposable egg cartons also make good molds.

❖ When frozen, microwave for a few seconds, unmold, and place the treats in a plastic bag and store in the freezer. (Note: if using Styrofoam egg cartons or cups, rest the containers briefly in a partially-filled pan of warm water to loosen contents. Unless the Styrofoam is labeled as microwave safe, it could melt.) If you want to be fancy, bone- and paw-shaped molds are available.

❖ Variation from Heather: When the concoction is half frozen, take out and roll in crumbled dog biscuits; serve then or place in zippered bag and return to freezer to save for later.

Contributor's Note from M.j: My dogs love these, especially in the summer. (Photo by M.j. above)

Contributor's Note from Maria: Great all-natural treat when treat time rolls around or your doggie needs a yummy cool-down on a hot day, just crack the trays to release.

Contributor's Note from Heather: We used this recipe for the first time a month ago and our dogs ate the entire first batch in a single day. - Needless to say, they loved it!

When you find a good deal on bananas, peel them, pop them in a zippered bag, then freeze for later use!

Dogs have given us their absolute all. We are the center of their universe. We are the focus of their love and faith and trust. They serve us in return for scraps. It is without a doubt the best deal man has ever made. ~ Roger Caras

Sweet Potato Yummies
Contributed by cstironkat

1 large sweet potato, cooked
½ cup blueberries
1 banana, mashed
1 cup apples, pared and chopped
1 cup green beans
1 ½ cups peanut butter
Apple juice or chicken broth, as needed

❖ Mix all ingredients and add enough apple juice or chicken broth to make and form small balls.

❖ Freeze.

Contributor's Note: My dogs love these on a hot day or as a special autumn treat.

Dogs are us, only innocent. ~ Cynthia Heimel

Banana Pup Pops
Contributed by cstironkat

1 quart carrot or apple juice (do not use grape juice if you substitute)
1 ripe banana, mashed
½ cup yogurt, plain or vanilla flavored

❖ Blend all ingredients and freeze.

Contributor's Note: My dogs love this cool treat in the summer.

Along with bananas, apple and melon make great frozen pops, too. Just be sure to remove the seeds!

A dog wags its tail with its heart.
~ Martin Buxbaum

PB & Carob Pupsicles
Contributed by Kelly Ann T.

1 cup yogurt (use plain or vanilla)
½ cup peanut butter
¼ cup carob chips*

❖ Whirl it all in a blender and then freeze in ice cube trays.

* Reminder: Carob is safe for dogs to eat; chocolate is not.

Contributor's Note: My dogs love this recipe, and I add banana and blueberries for extra flavor too.

Dogs are miracles with paws.
~ Susan Ariel Rainbow Kennedy (attributed)

Beefsicle Frozen Dog Treat
Contributed by DogTipper.com

1 pound ground beef
1 cup peas (fresh, canned or frozen)
7 cups water (divided)

❖ Put hamburger meat, peas, and TWO cups of water in the blender or food processor. Mix on low then increase the speed to liquefy the mixture. Add one more cup of water and continue to liquefy. Allow the mixture to liquefy a minute or two; this will spin off much of the fat of the ground beef. (You'll see a white film of fat building up on the inside of the blender).

❖ Pour the mixture into a 10-quart saucepan. Discard fat clinging to the blender.

❖ Add the remaining four cups of water. Cook on high until the water reaches a boil then reduce the heat to medium and allow it to cook at a slow boil for about half an hour. Remove from heat.

❖ After the mixture has cooled for about half an hour, pour the mixture into plastic tubs or glasses. I used a soup ladle to fill each tub a little more than half full. If you have a small dog, ice cube trays would be a good option, too.

As familiar with me as my dog.
~ William Shakespeare

Cool Yogurt Pup Cups
Contributed by Ruby's mom

1 cup mashed, ripe banana
½ cup low-fat, Greek-style yogurt
2 tablespoons natural peanut butter
little "Dixie" paper drinking cups

❖ Place small paper cups on a baking sheet.

❖ Combine banana and peanut butter, stir in yogurt. Pour into paper cups and fill to top. Place baking sheet with filled cups into freezer for at least 4 hours.

❖ Once frozen, put pup cups into freezer bag for storage. Hot day? Treat time? Pull one out of the freezer, tear off paper cup, and give to your dog. (Ruby licks hers right out of the cup; it's a little cleaner)

❖ Variations: I change this up and you can have so much fun doing the same using your pet's favorite things to eat. My girl loves carrots and broccoli so I hide those in the mix for chunky surprises. One of our (yes, "our") faves is mango, banana and yogurt. Just make your mixture, for example, 1 cup fruit or vegetable mash to ½ cup yogurt. You can stuff this mix into their Kongs, too. You can use ice cube trays, popsicle molds, etc.

Contributor's Note: Ruby is a five-year-old mixed breed. She loves to go hiking, to run, and to wade in the river for sticks. She attends an assisted living facility to visit the residents. She loves to learn, and to go down the slide at the park. Her favorite things are meeting new people, seeing her human and dog friends, and doing tricks for treats.

No one in your family will ever be as forgiving of your mistakes as your dog. ~ Susan Hyde

Ice Treats
Contributed by Barb U.

3-4 beef bouillon cubes
2 cups hot water

Make your own frozen bouillon cubes by cooking skin, bones, and leftover meat. Strain and refrigerate then skim off fat before freezing.

❖ I take 3-4 beef bouillon cubes and thoroughly mix them in 1-2 cups of hot water.

❖ I then pour the mixture into an ice cube tray. If any is left over, I mix it into some dry dog food as an extra treat.

❖ Let the mixture freeze, then I give them to my dogs as a treat on hot summer days.

❖ They know what's coming and get really excited. I haven't tried chicken yet, but pretty sure that would work just as well.

Contributor's Note: This is something I've been doing for years. A few years back I had dropped some ice cubes on the floor and after investigating them, my dogs picked them up and enjoyed them. I gave them plain ice cubes for a while, then one day had some extra beef bouillon broth left over and figured I'd freeze that for them. They loved them so much I've kept it up.

You can judge a man's true character by the way he treats his fellow animals. ~ Paul McCartney

Yogurt Bites
Contributed by Parsimonious Pash,
parsimoniouspash.com

Plain Yogurt

❖ Line the pan with the wax paper then you can choose which option you like. Normally I am lazy and just use a spoon and scoop then dollop it onto the sheet in neat little rows.

❖ The other way is to put the yogurt in a plastic bag and then cut the corner and make neat little drops. Put these in the freezer; once solid, you can transfer them into a container to keep in the freezer.

❖ These are great in the summer and cheaper than buying doggie ice cream from the store!

Contributor's Note: I love my pets like crazy and spoil them so I am always trying to find a way to make new little treats for them. I am a blog owner and I love finding and doing reviews on products for my pets! You can check it out here: parsimoniouspash.com

Brothsicles
Contributed by DogTipper.com

12 cups water
1 pound chicken breasts

- ❖ Cook the chicken breasts overnight in the slow cooker. If you used whole chicken breasts, you'll need to remove the bones from the mix and discard. When you're done, return the chicken to the broth.

- ❖ Stir the mixture well. The chicken will settle in the bottom of the broth so I stirred it between making each brothsicle so each frozen treat includes bits of chicken. Using a soup ladle, scoop and pour the broth mixture into plastic cups or ice cube trays.

- ❖ I put two scoops in each plastic cup but the size will depend on your dog's size. Pop the plastic cups in the freezer and wait a few hours then the treats are ready! If you used plastic cups, just run some warm water over the outside of the cups and the treats will pop right out.

DogTipper Note: Not only does this provide an inexpensive and tasty summer treat for your dog but it's also a good way to encourage your dog to consume extra water on hot days!

He is your friend, your partner, your defender, your dog. You are his life, his love, his leader. He will be yours, faithful and true, to the last beat of his heart. You owe it to him to be worthy of such devotion. ~ Unknown

Fido's Frozen Fruit Pupsicle
Contributed by DogTipper.com

4 cups water
1 tablespoon molasses dissolved in the water (optional)
1 cup fresh fruit (NOT grapes or raisins), chopped

- ❖ For the fruit, I used a couple of strawberries, a handful of blueberries, and some local peaches which are in season here right now. (Always discard peach pits; they're toxic to dogs if they chew on them as are some other fruit pits such as apricots and plums. If you use apples, discard the seeds for the same reason.)

- ❖ You can freeze the mix in ice cube trays; I used six plastic tubs I had stored away. Fill each with about an inch of the water/molasses mixture then drop in some of the fruit. Freeze.

If you want a friend in Washington, get a dog.
~ Harry S. Truman

Did You Say Bacon? Pupsicles
Contributed by Kirby the Dorkie,
www.kirbythedorkie.com

1 cup plain yogurt
4-ounce cup cinnamon applesauce
¼ cup milk
3 tablespoons maple syrup*
3-ounce bag real bacon bits

❖ In a measuring cup with spout, thoroughly mix together all of the ingredients except the bacon.

❖ Stir in the bacon. Pour the mixture into molds or ice cube trays. Cover with plastic wrap and let freeze for 4 to 6 hours.

❖ Twist to remove. If they won't come out easily, hold bottom of molds under cool running water and then twist.

* I used real maple syrup. Pancake syrup would have too many added ingredients.

Holiday Treats

Pumpkin Dog Treats
Contributed by M.j.

1 (15-ounce) can mashed pure pumpkin NOTE: Do not use spiced pie filling
¾ cup cream of wheat*
½ cup dry powdered milk
Unsweetened carob chips

* or rice cereal if your dog is sensitive to wheat

- ❖ Preheat oven to 300 degrees F.

- ❖ Mix all ingredients. Using an inexpensive pastry bag (available at your grocery store), make 1½- to 2-inch swirls or rosettes onto a lightly-greased cookie sheet.

- ❖ In the center of each swirl, drop a carob chip. Treats come out soft and slightly chewy.

- ❖ Bake for 15-20 minutes. Cool before serving or storing.

Contributor's Note: My dogs love pumpkin.

Don't accept your dog's admiration as conclusive evidence that you are wonderful. ~ Ann Landers

Thanksgiving Treats
Contributed by The Beals Dogs,
TheBealsDogs.blogspot.com

2 cups cooked turkey, diced
4 teaspoons grated cheese
1 tablespoon parsley, freshly
chopped
2 eggs
2 cups whole wheat flour
2 tablespoons brewers yeast
2 tablespoons vegetable oil

❖ Preheat oven to 350 degrees F.

❖ Combine turkey, cheese, parsley and mix well. Beat the eggs in a bowl and pour over turkey mixture. Add the flour, brewer's yeast, and oil.

❖ Stir until thoroughly mixed and all ingredients are coated. Drop into small lumps onto ungreased cookie sheet.

❖ Bake for about 20 minutes, until brown and firm.

❖ Store in refrigerator.

Contributor's Note: The Beals dogs are Mystique 'Tiki', Colossus & Magneto, Siberian Huskies that LOVE treats! Their blog is TheBealsDogs.blogspot.com. This is their favorite treat around Thanksgiving time.

Turkey & Sweet Potato Treats
Contributed by cstironkat

6 ounces ground turkey
½ cup apples
1 cup cooked sweet potato
4 tablespoons whole wheat flour

- ❖ Preheat oven to 350 degrees F.

- ❖ Puree meat and apples in a food processor. Mix all ingredients.

- ❖ Roll into 1-inch balls. Bake until browned then cool before serving or storing.

Contributor's Note: My dogs love these treats and they are perfect for Thanksgiving.

The censure of a dog is something no man can stand. ~ Christopher Morley

PB & Pumpkin Dog Cookies
Contributed by Murphy's Momma

2½ cups whole wheat flour
2 eggs
½ cup canned pure
pumpkin*
2 tablespoons peanut butter
½ teaspoon salt
½ teaspoon ground
cinnamon

*I use 1 cup pumpkin and
add ½ cup oatmeal; can use
quick cooking or old-
fashioned

❖ Preheat oven to 350 degrees F.

❖ Mix all ingredients together. May add more peanut butter and water if mixture is too dry. You don't want it too wet, but you want it to stick together.

❖ Roll dough into a log as big as you want then slice off into pieces. You may want to wrap log in plastic wrap and freeze for a few minutes to make slicing easier.

❖ Bake until firm, about 40 minutes. Cool completely and store in freezer.

❖ You can make these treats tiny as tiny training treats by rolling the log skinnier. Baking time will be shorter with smaller treats.

Contributor's Note: I love baking for my dogs!!!

Precious Penelope Peanut's
Pumpkin Pie Tasty Treats
Contributed by Murphy's Momma

1 ½ cups whole wheat flour
2 cups all purpose flour-plus extra for rolling
½ cup rolled or old fashioned oats
1 teaspoon ground cinnamon
1 teaspoon ground nutmeg
½ cup chicken broth
¾ cup canned pumpkin (solid pumpkin-not pumpkin pie mix)
1 tablespoon oil
1 tablespoon maple syrup
1 egg

❖ Preheat oven to 350 degrees F.

❖ In large bowl, combine dry ingredients. In a separate bowl, combine remaining ingredients.

❖ Add wet ingredients to dry and mix well. Use hands to incorporate all the flour in.

❖ Roll out on floured surface to ½-inch thickness.

❖ Cut into biscuits and place on greased foil-covered cookie sheet. Bake 30 to 40 minutes or until brown. Store in airtight container in the fridge.

Contributor's Note: Tips: I use my bread maker to mix all ingredients and make the dough. Then I roll in balls and smash with a glass or using a fork like peanut butter cookies. Then I leave my dog cookies in oven as it's cooling to make them even crisper. I also store my dog treats in the freezer for a cold, crunchy snack!

Whosoever loveth me loveth my hound.
~ Sir Thomas More

St. Patty's Day Patties
contributed by DogTipper.com

For the Labs and Lassies in your home!

1 ½ cups all-purpose flour
1 cup whole wheat flour
2 teaspoons baking powder
4 strips bacon, cut into small pieces
4 cups green peas, drained (about two cans)
2 tablespoons water

❖ Preheat oven to 325 degrees F.

❖ Mix dry ingredients. Fry bacon and reserve drippings; cool. Put peas in blender or food processor and blend. Mix blended peas and bacon with drippings; add dry ingredients and mix well.

❖ Knead dough and pat out or roll to under ½ inch thickness. Cut with cookie cutters to desired shape and place on lightly oiled cookie sheet. Bake for 25 minutes or until browned. Cool and serve.

Pumpkin Sticks
Contributed by Doodlebug

1 can pure pumpkin
1 ½ cups rice flour
¾ cup flax seeds
2 teaspoon cinnamon

❖ Preheat oven to 350 degrees F.

❖ Mix all ingredients then roll into ½-inch sticks. Bake on cookie sheets for 25 minutes.

❖ Refrigerate for up to 2 weeks.

Contributor's Note: My Jack loves his pumpkin treats. I have had Jack for three years after I found him in a shelter one day away from being put down. He is an American Staffordshire/ Shar-Pei/Dalmation mix and my spoiled rotten sweetie. Fair warning....your dog may jump on the counter to get at these treats because they smell wonderful!

The more I see of men, the more I like dogs.
~ Madame De Stael

Murphy's Fave Apple Pie Cookies
Contributed by Murphy's Momma

1 cup chopped apple (can leave the skin on but make sure it's cored and no seeds remain)
1 teaspoon cinnamon
1 cup water
½ cup vegetable oil
1 cup powdered milk
5 cups flour*
2 large eggs

*I use a mix of unbleached white and whole wheat flour.

- ❖ Preheat oven to 350 degrees F.

- ❖ Using hands, mix all ingredients together.

- ❖ Turn out onto floured counter top and knead well. May need more flour if dough is too sticky. Roll out thin and cut with cookie cutters.

- ❖ Bake 20-25 minutes until browned. Leave out to dry/harden well. Refrigerate for a week or in freezer to keep longer.

Contributor's Note: I usually double this recipe and it makes a quite a lot! Then I freeze them and give them out at Christmas to our friends with dogs along with homemade seafoam candy for the people. This recipe makes the whole house smell wonderful!!!

My Collie Murphy LOVES apples. We have two small apple trees in our yard, or I should say Murphy has two apple trees and he checks them daily during the growing season until we tell him OK, get the apple! Then he stands on his hind legs and gently picks an apple. After the required game of keep away, he lies down to eat his apple.

The language of friendship is not words but meanings. ~ Henry David Thoreau

Easter Carrot Cake Cookies
Contributed by DogTipper.com

2 cups rolled oats
2 cups all-purpose flour
1 cup grated carrots
2 tablespoons molasses
½ cup (1 stick) butter,
softened
2 large eggs
2 teaspoons baking powder
½ cup water

For filling: 4 ounces cream
cheese, softened (optional)

❖ Preheat oven to 350 degrees F.

❖ Mix all ingredients except cream cheese; combine well until completely mixed. Roll dough on a lightly floured surface to ¼-inch thickness and cut into cookie shapes. Bake for approximately 30 minutes until browned. Remove cookies from oven and cool completely.

❖ After the cookies are cooled, you can make some of them extra-special by turning them into a sandwich, with a layer of softened cream cheese between two cookies. Refrigerate the treats with the cream cheese filling (and the others, too, if you won't be serving them for a few days).

With both the plain and filled version, you'll be making your four-legged friend very happy with these hoppy treats!

Fido's Fruitcake
Contributed by DogTipper.com

2 cups all-purpose flour
1 cup fresh cranberries
⅓ cup molasses
1 cup pecans, divided
1 apple, peeled and cored
1 egg
1 teaspoon baking powder
1 teaspoon cinnamon
1 cup water

Wonder if your baking powder is too old? Add 1 teaspoon to a cup of hot tap water. If it doesn't fizz, toss it out!

❖ Preheat oven to 350 degrees F and grease muffin pans.

❖ Chop cranberries, apple, and half the pecans in a food processor or blender. In a large bowl, combine all other ingredients; when mixed, add cranberry-apple-pecan mixture and stir. Pour (heavy) batter into the muffin pans.

❖ If you don't have pecans, any other nut except macadamia nuts will work, too (macadamia nuts are toxic for dogs).

❖ Bake for about half an hour then cool completely before serving and refrigerating. Save one for Santa!

Cranberry Dog Treats
Contributed by DogTipper.com

2 cups whole wheat flour
2 cups all-purpose flour
1 cup oats
¼ cup molasses
1 cup cranberries
1 egg
½ stick (4 tablespoons) butter, melted
1 teaspoon cinnamon
1 teaspoon baking powder
½ cup water, as needed

❖ Preheat oven to 350 degrees F and grease two cookie sheets.

❖ Toss the cranberries into a blender or food processor and chop. Mix all the dry ingredients in a large bowl then add the melted butter, chopped cranberries, egg, and, slowly, the water a little bit at a time.

❖ Mix the dough and knead on a lightly floured surface, rolling the dough to about ¼-inch thick. Use cookie cutters to cut into desired shapes.

❖ Place the treats on the baking sheet, leaving just a little room between each.

❖ Pop the cookie sheets in the oven and bake for 30 minutes. At the end of baking, turn off the oven and allow the treats to cool in the oven for about three or four hours to make treats crunchy. Once the treats have completely cooled, you can serve them or refrigerate them.

Turkey & Cranberry Treats
Contributed by DogTipper.com

1 cup whole cranberries
1 cup cooked, boned turkey
3 ½ cups whole wheat flour
1 egg
1 tablespoon baking powder
1 tablespoon olive oil
½ cup water or broth as needed

❖ Preheat oven to 350 degrees and lightly grease two cookie sheets.

❖ Mix the dry ingredients in a large mixing bowl. In a blender or food processor, add the turkey and egg (and some of the water or broth as needed). When the turkey is the consistency of baby food, add cranberries and continue to mix.

❖ Pour this mixture into the mixing bowl with the dry ingredients and stir to create a thick dough.

❖ On a lightly floured surface, knead the dough. (This is a heavy dough so you'll need to put a little muscle in it!)

❖ Cut into biscuit shapes and bake for 25 minutes. Cool completely before serving or refrigerating.

For me a house or an apartment becomes a home when you add one set of four legs, a happy tail, and that indescribable measure of love we call a dog. ~ Roger Caras

Witchy Chicken Fingers
Contributed by DogTipper.com

This is a canine variation of the ever-popular Witches' Fingers cookie for humans but our doggie recipe is simpler, substituting the sugars and flavorings with savory chicken and the red decorating gel with plain old molasses.

2 cups all-purpose flour
1 ½ cups whole wheat flour
1 ½ cups cooked chicken
1 egg
1 tablespoon molasses
1 teaspoon baking powder
Almonds

❖ Preheat oven to 350 degrees F and grease a cookie sheet.

❖ Whether you use boiled or canned chicken, start by tossing the chicken in the blender or food processor and blending until it has the consistency of baby food. (Or you could really save time and just use a couple of jars of baby food if you like. Always make sure the baby food has NO onion powder, though.)

❖ Mix together chicken, egg, and baking powder. Add this chicken mixture to the flours and knead the dough.

❖ Now it's time for the fun part: shaping the fingers! Pinch off about a ping pong ball-sized piece of dough and start rolling it between your palms to make a tube of dough about four inches long. Roll it to about finger thickness then place on cookie sheet.

❖ Use the molasses to paint a little spot beneath the "fingernail"…it will ooze out from beneath the almond "nail" and look a little like blood…so don't worry about this being perfect. Place a single almond (the tip of the almond should be pointing out, like a spiky fingernail) and press down just a little to secure the almond in the dough.

❖ Bake about 20-25 minutes and you're done! Cool the treats completely before serving or refrigerating.

PB & Pumpkin Treats
contributed by DogTipper.com

2 ½ cups whole wheat flour
½ cup pumpkin
½ cup peanut butter (organic if you have it)
2 teaspoons cinnamon
1 teaspoon baking powder
½ cup water as needed

❖ Preheat oven to 350 degrees F.

❖ The pumpkin you'll need is canned pumpkin…but NOT pumpkin pie filling (which has too many spices and too much sugar). You're looking for just plain canned pumpkin.

❖ Mix all your ingredients except the water then add it sparingly. Depending on the amount of oil in your peanut butter, you may need the entire ½ cup…or not. The dough should turn out sticky but not dry; if it feels dry, you need a little more water. If it's too sticky, add a little more flour.

❖ Roll the dough on a lightly floured surface and cut into fun shapes.

Bake on cookie sheets for about 20 minutes then remove and cool. Be sure to cool the treats completely before serving or refrigerating. And be warned: the smell of these treats baking is frighteningly good! You just might have to test one before giving it to your dog!

A dog believes you are what you think you are.
~ Jane Swan

Other Treats

Claudia's Homemade Dog Treats
Contributed by Claudia M.

1 cup Cream of Wheat (Dry)
1 cup Carnation Dry Milk (low-fat) (Dry)
One jar organic carrot baby food
One jar organic turkey baby food (or any other flavor your dog loves such as chicken, beef, etc.)

❖ Preheat oven to 350 degrees F.

❖ Mix together ingredients. Drop onto a parchment-lined cookie sheet in the size you desire.

❖ Bake until lightly browned on edges. Cool.

Contributor's Note: YoYo, our Min-pin we rescued out of a ferret cage, just loves those treats.

For Better or for Wurst
Contributed by ToCo

½ cup liverwurst
¼ cup mashed potatoes (cooled)
¼ cup frozen peas

- ❖ Combine all the above; peas can remain frozen. Refrigerate.

- ❖ I usually give my two fur babies around four tablespoons each on every second day.

Contributor's Note: More of a staple than a treat, but believe me, to them it's a treat! Can be frozen if one would like. I use this as a treat three times a week, but it's more of a staple, and my two love it!

No matter how little money and how few possessions you own, having a dog makes you rich. ~ Louis Sabin

Cheese Poppers
Contributed by cstironkat

2 ⅓ cups whole wheat flour
¼ cup olive oil
½ cup grated cheddar cheese
1 egg
¼ cup powdered milk
Additional grated cheese for topping (optional)

❖ Preheat oven to 350 degrees F.

❖ Mix all ingredients. Roll out dough. Cut dough into desired shapes and sprinkle more grated cheese on top of poppers.

❖ Bake for 15 minutes. If you want hard poppers, leave off cheese on top and, after turning off oven, cool treats in oven overnight.

Contributor's Note: My dogs love cheese. I keep these in the frig after baking.

Dogs laugh, but they laugh with their tails.
~ Max Eastman

Dinner for a Princess
Contributed by Shelly PoochParkWear

½ pound chicken, turkey, and/or beef
2 carrots, diced
1 sweet potato, peeled
1 apple, pared and cored
½ cup cooked brown rice (optional)

❖ Boil meat in pot. In a separate pot, boil vegetables and apple (or have these cooked in advance.) In a separate pot, boil brown rice (or have pre-cooked).

❖ When cooked, cool meat, vegetables, and rice.

❖ Chop meats.

❖ With hand blender, blend the rice and veggies/apple until pureed; add to the meat. Mix all ingredients with some of the stock from the meat. Serve.

Contributor's Note: Layla and Baby R.I.P. did not eat kibbles so this is what I fed them and they loved it.

Love me, love my dog.
~ Saint Bernard of Clairvaux

Plantain & Pork Balls
Contributed by Lynda Castillo

2 green plantains (not yet ripe, still green and firm)
8 strips bacon, chopped

- ❖ Peel the plantains. Boil the plantains until soft (not too soft, though; it's like cooking a potato).

- ❖ Remove from water and mash up a bit; again you don't want mush.

- ❖ Fry bacon. Reserve some of the remaining bacon grease. Throw in mashed plantain and bacon bits and mix it up.

- ❖ Let flavors come out; leave covered on low heat for a couple minutes. Let cool enough to handle, then form into bite-size balls.

Contributor's Note: My late beloved dog used to love these. I had originally made it as a side dish for our lunch or dinner and decided to simplify the recipe and form them into balls for my dog to enjoy as a treat.

Every dog has his day.
~ English proverb

Peppy Honey PB Carob Chip Snacks
Contributed by Peppy Paws dog walking

2 tablespoons corn oil
½ cup peanut butter
1 cup water
1 cup whole wheat flour
2 cups all-purpose flour
½ cup MINI carob chips
2 tablespoons honey

- ❖ Preheat oven to 350 degrees F.

- ❖ Combine oil, peanut butter, honey and water. Add flour, one cup at a time, then knead until firm.

- ❖ Roll dough to ¼-inch thickness and cut with cookie cutter. Place on an ungreased cookie sheet and bake for 20 minutes.

- ❖ Makes 2½ dozen (give or take).

Approved by Rascalini the wonder belly!

Contributor's Note: I own Peppy Paws dog walking and I make these for my clients. I have had several clients tell me that these are their dogs' favorite treats and if I can please make more!

A dog is the only thing on earth that loves you more than you love yourself. ~ Josh Billings

Drool Gruel

Contributed by E. Weaver

½ cup rolled oats
½ teaspoon chia seeds
1 tablespoon non-hydrogenated margarine
1 tablespoon slivered almonds
⅛ cup blueberries or apple chunks
1 ½ cups water or unsweetened almond milk

❖ Place oats and water (or almond milk) in a small pot and bring to a boil. Reduce to a simmer and stir frequently while adding chia seeds, margarine, almonds, and fruit.

❖ Continue to stir as it simmers until the mixture is creamy.

❖ Allow to cool, but not completely; your dog will especially enjoy this treat if it is still a little warm, and he is coming in from the cold.

Contributor's Note: E. Weaver has a dog who loves raw carrots.

All knowledge, the totality of all questions and all answers, is contained in the dog. ~ Franz Kafka

Canine Crouton Treats
Contributed by DogTipper.com

6 slices bread
½ cup bacon fat (or substitute olive or other oil or melted butter)
½ cup grated Parmesan cheese

❖ Preheat oven to 250 degrees F.

❖ Cut the bread in one-inch squares. Toss the bread squares with the Parmesan cheese.

❖ Drizzle the bread with the oil. When you're done, just pop it on a cookie sheet (no need to grease it!) and bake for 30-40 minutes. I turned the croutons twice to make sure they browned evenly.

❖ When the croutons are browned, remove them from the oven and allow them to cool before refrigerating or serving. Our dogs really liked these treats!

Chicken & Kibble Cupcakes
Contributed by DogTipper.com

This recipe makes a fun way to use the kibble "dust" left at the bottom of a big sack!

1 cup cooked chicken
3 cups dry dog food (kibble) of your choice
1 ½ cups chicken broth
1 teaspoon baking powder
2 eggs

❖ Preheat oven to 350 degrees F. Grease cupcake pans.

❖ Grind the kibble. I used the blender, grinding just a cup of dog food at a time. (If you have a clean coffee grinder, that will work, too.) Once the kibble is crushed, pour all dry ingredients in a large bowl.

❖ Put chicken and chicken broth in the blender and mix. Add chicken and chicken broth mixture to the dry ingredients and mix. The mix is heavy; you won't be able to pour it in the cupcake pans.

❖ Using a teaspoon, scoop a large spoonful of mixture into your hands, compressing and shaping it like meatballs. Drop the "meatball" into the cupcake tray, slightly press it into position, and repeat until you're done.

❖ Bake for 20 minutes. Allow treats to cool completely before serving or refrigerating.

Kibble Cupcakes
Contributed by DogTipper.com

2 cups kibble or kibble dust
1 cup whole wheat flour
1 cup shredded cheese
1 cup water
2 tablespoons olive oil
1 tablespoon baking powder

Did you know?

The bag your kibble comes in is a safe form of food storage. Use a clip to keep it sealed. Once opened, use the food within about six weeks.

❖ Preheat oven to 350 degrees F.

❖ If you have plenty of kibble dust, you can jump right into mixing your ingredients; if, like me, you've got a mix of dust and kibble, you'll need to break it all up a little first. A clean coffee bean grinder is great for this or try your blender or food processor.

❖ Mix all the ingredients. Pop the muffin pans into the oven for about half an hour or until the muffins are slightly browned on top (and a little browner on the bottom).

❖ Cool the treats completely before serving and before refrigerating.

To err is human, to forgive canine.
~ Anonymous

Appendix: Oven Temperatures

Fahrenheit (F)	Celsius (C)
225 degrees F	110 degrees C
250 degrees F	130 degrees C
275 degrees F	140 degrees C
300 degrees F	150 degrees C
325 degrees F	165 degrees C
350 degrees F	177 degrees C
375 degrees F	190 degrees C
400 degrees F	200 degrees C
425 degrees F	220 degrees C
450 degrees F	230 degrees C
475 degrees F	245 degrees C
500 degrees F	260 degrees C
550 degrees F	290 degrees C

Appendix: Conversion Chart

U.S. Volume	Metric Volume (ml/l)
1/4 teaspoon	1.23 ml
1/2 teaspoon	2.5 ml
3/4 teaspoon	3.7 ml
1 teaspoon	4.9 ml
1 1/2 teaspoons (1/2 tablespoon)	7.5 ml
2 teaspoons	10 ml
3 teaspoons (1 tablespoon)	15 ml
1/8 cup (2 tablespoons/1 ounce)	30 ml
1/4 cup (4 tablespoons/2 ounces)	60 ml
1/2 cup (8 tablespoons/4 ounces)	120 ml
3/4 cup (12 tablespoons/6 ounces)	180 ml
1 cup (16 tablespoons/8 ounces)	240 ml

About DogTipper.com

Founded in 2008 by professional writers Paris Permenter and John Bigley, DogTipper.com focuses on saving money and saving dogs. The award-winning site features tips, adoptable dogs, dog news, product reviews, giveaways, and more.

In 2012, DogTipper.com was named Best Dog Blog in the BlogPaws awards in Salt Lake City; months later, the site also received a Petties award for Best Use of Social Media in the DogTime annual awards.

Along with My Dog Says I'm a Great Cook!™, DogTipper.com also publishes *Barkonomics: Tips for Frugal Fidos* with over 300 ways to save money on your dog's care and *The Dog and Cat Rescue Coloring and Activity Book*, a fun way to introduce children to the joy of adopting a pet.

For more information on DogTipper, visit www.dogtipper.com and follow on social media on Twitter at @dogtipper and Facebook at www.facebook.com/dogtipper.

About Paris Permenter
& John Bigley

Paris Permenter and John Bigley are a husband-wife team of professional writers and the publishers of DogTipper.com. The pet parents of two rescue dogs, Tiki and Irie, Paris and John launched DogTipper.com in 2008.

Paris and John are the authors of nearly 30 published books including *Barkonomics: Tips for Frugal Fidos*. The couple has a long history of frugal living, starting with the launch of their writing business. As America's Pet Economist™, Paris speaks at pet expos across the country on the topic of saving money on pet care and has been an expert source on the subject for articles in publications ranging from *Woman's Day* to The Huffington Post.

Paris and John live in the country with their dogs and cats in the Texas Hill Country.